CANADIAN ENTRY

CANADIAN

ENTRY

by *Christilot Hanson*

Preface by Waldemar Seunig

FOLLETT PUBLISHING COMPANY

Chicago New York

Library of Congress Catalog Card Number: 66-30000
Follett Publishing Company
1010 West Washington Boulevard
Chicago, Illinois 60607

T 1030

Printed in Canada

To Bonheur

the horse that made this story possible

Illustrations

Following pages 54 and 70 there are photographs illustrating the phases of Christilot's career, the exercises described in the Appendix, and the execution of some dressage movements.

Contents

		Page
	Preface	
1	Dancing Years	3
2	The Horses in My Life	18
3	Anatole	34
4	First Trip to Germany	45
5	The *Reitinstitut*	59
6	Show Riding	79
7	Tokyo 1964!	99
	Appendix: A Free Dancer's Approach to Dressage	129
	Glossary of Dressage Terms	139

Acknowledgments

The photographs on page 1 of the illustrated section are by Lloyd Studio, Singapore (left) and Reg Innell (right) ; page 2 by Ken Bell; page 3 by Ramon Stringer; page 4 by Toronto *Telegram* (top left) and Doug Boult Art Associates (bottom left) : page 6 by Budd, New York; pages 8 to 12 by Robert C. Ragsdale, except page 11 (top).

Preface

It seems to me most extraordinary that a teen-age girl should spend long hours, days and years of her life in the saddle in order to represent her country worthily at the Olympics, in competition with the world's riding elite. Yet from early childhood Christilot Hanson devoted herself with single-minded dedication to this end and accomplished the unique feat brilliantly and with great distinction.

Christilot is richly endowed with mental and physical advantages by her parents, who come of good Eurasian, Romanic and Anglo-Saxon stock. She has been able, moreover, to develop her inherited talents to the full under the guidance of masters of the classic art of riding, since her mother has seen to it that she has the very best teachers available.

Christilot describes in her book the road she followed in pursuit of her goal, a road that led her over three continents, "exalted to the heights of joy or plunged into the depths of despair"—for fate does not strew roses only. *Canadian Entry* is an endearing work, written by a clear-eyed young person who combines a thoughtfulness far beyond her years with a refreshing sense of humour. It is a true portrayal of the life of a young rider who has been transported by the thrill of breathtaking motion and the steely melody of flying hooves—an experience which gives the rider a strong character, a sense of rapport with his horse, and an understanding of that noble animal's innermost being.

A famous master of manège, when asked about his method, once said, "Feeling is everything." Christilot has proven the truth of this statement. Because she is thoroughly familiar with her mother's style of free-form expressive dancing, Christilot's performances are examples of elegant, apparently effortless self-discipline. Her dream of a floating dance on horseback, winged by harmony, has come true. Yet this Terpsichore of dressage is not one-sided. Her soaring flight over difficult jumps is a joy to behold and testifies to initiate and uninitiate alike that she is well versed in all forms of the sport.

For me, knowing authors, riders and horses of many lands, it was a highlight to meet Christilot, Bonheur and their book.

July, 1966   WALDEMAR SEUNIG
Translated from the German

CANADIAN ENTRY

"Determine that the thing can and shall be done, and then we shall find a way."

ABRAHAM LINCOLN,
Speech in Congress,
June 20, 1848.

1 Dancing years

I was born in Batavia, on the island of Java, ten minutes after midnight on April 12, 1947. My mother, a choreographer, had always looked forward to having a child of her own, who would, of course, be a dancer! She expected her baby to be beautiful, graceful and fine-boned. . . .

When the huge Dutch midwife showed me to her, Mother closed her eyes and murmured: "Take it away." I was bright pink, stocky and definitely not "fine-boned." But the unwelcome reception did not perturb me in the least. I am told that I let my hunger be known at once in no uncertain terms. I suppose that, as the weeks went by, Mother became accustomed to me and decided to do the best with what she had.

My father was in his native land of Australia at the time, looking for a home for us. Having become entranced with the East, however, he finally decided that we should settle in Singapore. So at the age of three months, I was taken by boat from Java to Singapore to the house that would be home for the next four years.

Mother engaged two Cantonese "amahs," one to cook and do the housework and one to look after me. Although I do not remember anything until I was three, pictures in the family scrapbook make it all too plain that I was not the skinniest of babies. I had three breakfasts, three lunches and three dinners a day. The first was my own, the second was with the amahs, who fed me mouthfuls of rice with their own chopsticks to keep me happy, and the third was with Father and Mother, who were served their meals separately at a later hour. With me becoming daily less sylph-like, Mother in her desperation began exercising me from my twelfth month on.

I was a silent child, not given to making much noise. However, I made up for this lack with a tremendous amount of movement. On waking I would immediately get up and rock the carriage that I had been sleeping in, causing it to tip forward and spill me out. This period of my life was marked with perpetual bumps and bruises. I didn't know then that this was one phase I would never outgrow.

When the time came for me to play with toys, my parents found that I much preferred animals. They gave me a little schnauzer pup that I adored. It had been with us only a short time when a dog belonging to our next door neighbour bit it fatally. Mother and Dad did not dare tell me what had happened. After I had plagued them with questions about the whereabouts of my pet, which they artfully evaded, they were shocked to find that I was running a high fever. The doctor diagnosed my case as an emotional upset of some kind and, hearing about the pup, suggested that Father and Mother buy me a new one. There were no puppies left at the kennel, but the breeder sold us a full-grown collie that had been imported from Australia, where it had helped a farmer herd sheep. As soon as I was shown the dog, the fever subsided and the collie gave up sheep-herding to become my playmate. I named him "Pataud," after the puppy I had lost.

Caged with Pataud at the kennel was a female collie, called "Dixy." Mother preferred Dixy to Pataud because she was exceptionally beautiful, but the breeder would not part with her. A month later we received a call from the breeder, who asked if we were still interested in Dixy. A visit to the kennels disclosed the reason why we had been offered the dog. Dixy was dying from homesickness. It appeared that she had been shipped from Australia as a full-grown collie. Mother took pity on the creature with the sad, shining eyes, confident that she could nurse Dixy back to life.

Little by little, after months of being hand-fed, the sick dog once more became her usual, beautiful self. She became so attached to Mother that she would not even eat when Mother left the house. Sometimes she consented to go for a walk with Amah, Pataud and me in the Botanical Gardens. I still remember the fun we had chasing the monkeys that lived free in the trees. Pataud was much faster than Amah at tracking me down and keeping me within the confines of the Gardens. He saw to it that I did not wander off to roam the streets as I had sometimes done before.

I never saw much of Daddy while we were living in Singapore, because he worked on a rubber plantation in the jungle. It was too dangerous for us to join him. Chinese Communists camping in the surrounding area conducted numerous surprise attacks on the city. The planters carried revolvers all day. In the evenings the papers were full of stories of bus drivers having been shot dead in front of their passengers, with the killers walking calmly away and the police unable to get information from the frightened witnesses. It was hard to live a normal, relaxed life in this atmosphere of mass intimidation. Mother, scarcely recovered from the effects of the Japanese war, the Indonesian revolution in Java and my birth, found it impossible to bring up her child harmoniously in the way she had planned.

Then I guess that destiny helped her along. One day an ex-pupil turned up at our house. Did Mother still conduct dancing classes? No? But why not? Disturbing times or not, weight problems remained to be solved! Mother realized that her former pupil was right. She went on to reflect that continuous reports of terrorist activities induce a state of fear in people, which manifests itself in the body by a lack of spontaneous movement. Cultivation of spontaneous, natural movement releases nervous tension and enables a person to live normally in abnormal circumstances.

The pupil then arranged to bring a friend once a week to go through a routine of specially designed exercises. This friend, who was a staff writer on the local paper, reported the weekly sessions in *The Straits Times*. As a result, the telephone did not stop ringing and before Mother realized what had happened, she was conducting a full-fledged "Fine Art of Movement" school in her house.

As the work increased, Mother discovered that she had been sorely missing the profession that had occupied her before the war. Enthusiastically loading herself with work, she began planning her first recital. I used to sit with my legs crossed, watching the classes and rehearsals from an open doorway for hours on end, rocking to the beat of the music. I had barely outgrown the creeping stage. The "Frog Dance" from Hans Christian Andersen's fairy tale "The Tin Soldier" was the piece that appealed to me most. One day, when Mother was practising the tune on the piano at home, she was interrupted by the excited voice of the amah.

"Look Mem!" the amah cried, pointing at me. I was squatting in the corner, going through the whole dance. Mother

noticed that as soon as she stopped the music, I stopped dancing. When she resumed playing, I too would continue.
Quickly she realized that I associated the music with the
steps. Whenever anyone so much as hummed the frog
melody, I dropped whatever was occupying me and went
through the dance. It did not matter where it happened, at
home, in a shop, or in the street. So Mother got the idea to
experiment with me on the stage.

On the evening of the recital, the amah, rocking me in her
arms, stood waiting in the wings. When the moment came for
my dance, she proudly let me loose before the footlights. At
first the public thought it was a joke and laughed at the
toddler in the green leotard. The corners of my mouth began
to quiver. For a moment it seemed that I was going to cry.
"Oh no!" Mother thought. She motioned to the pianist to
begin. The first notes of the well known music caught my
ears. I flopped down into a squatting position in anticipation
of the tune, which, obligingly, began all over again. Everyone
sighed in relief as I went through the measures of my
dance.

A thundering applause was my reward. By this time I decided I liked being on stage, for I ignored Mother's beckon-
ing finger that was calling me back into the wings. But Amah
reacted quickly. Holding out a candy between her thumb
and first finger, she lured me backstage. Thus I made my
dance debut at the age of two at the Victoria Theatre in
Singapore. Since then Mother has called me "a professional
ham."

So my life enacted itself eventfully at home, in Mother's
school and on the stage, against an even more eventful background of happenings in the South Pacific. The Japanese,
after the war was over in Southeast Asia, had expressed the

opinion that although the United States had won the war from a military point of view, they had lost it politically. The slogan "Asia Bangun!", meaning "Asia Wake Up!", had caught on. Once a riot broke out in our street, during which the natives threw kerosene tins into the houses, hoping to see the English section of town go up in flames. Afterwards Mother said that she longed to move to a place where she could work without the misery of war.

Wherever Mother went, war seemed to follow. In 1938 she had been studying at the Hellerau-Laxenburg School of Free Movement in Vienna when the Germans marched into the city, forcing her and the other students to evacuate the former royal castle in which the school was conducted. The dancers and their professors had to relinquish it to "Tank Regiment No. 4," the commander of which was none other than General Hermann von Oppeln Bronikowski, the man who was to teach me dressage twenty-two years later! Mother moved to Prague, only to be followed by the German Army. From Prague she travelled to Paris and London, where she lived during the Blitz. She made her dance debut at the Aldwych Theatre under the most unnerving conditions. The dancers never knew when their performance might be cut short by wailing sirens. But her career came to an abrupt end when her parents, who owned a rubber and tea plantation in Java, called her back home. That was in 1940. In Bandung, the town of her birth, she established her first dance school.

In 1942 Japanese forces occupied Java, during which time Mother was jailed several times for feeding Dutch prisoners of war and hiding an Australian intelligence officer. This brought her in 1945 into contact with the Australian Army Headquarters—and with Father. They were married in 1946 in a ceremony conducted by an officer of Allied Supreme

Command. After I was born and we had made our home in Singapore instead of Australia, it became apparent that peace was not going to be realized for a long time. It was then that Mother and Dad decided to move to Canada.

Although we did our best to keep our departure from the Colony as secret as possible, quite a crowd turned out to bid us farewell. Newsmen, fellow dancers, pupils, friends, were all there with bouquets and baskets of flowers, and some with handkerchiefs. Weeping at the dockside was my amah, who had been a second mother to me. She was almost inconsolable at the thought of losing her small charge. She had been crying steadily from dawn the day before, vowing that she would never look after another child again. Before we sailed, however, she confided to Mother that she had a three-year-old boy to look after in her new job. But for the time being, it took quite a few people at the wharf to comfort her, as I cried "Goodbye Amah!" from the deck of our ship.

Quite worried about who would do the cooking for us from now on, I was relieved when the ship's dinner bell rang and I discovered that amahs were not the only people who could prepare meals. I even got rice, but without chopsticks. Luckily Mother had thought of bringing a pair, knowing she would have to accustom me slowly to eating the Western way.

Finally we arrived in Quebec on the *Franconia*, having come by way of Holland. We met Pataud two days later at Toronto Union Station. Seeing him again was like having a bit of Singapore with us. After we had taken a room in a hotel, Mother, with her typical direct approach, tackled the problem of finding a place to open a school.

While she was riding in a streetcar one day, a middle-aged, quiet, conservative-looking gentleman sitting opposite her overheard her use the word "tram." He asked her if she were a foreigner. When she said Yes, he enquired what she had come to do in Canada. Mother told him that she was a choreographer and wished to establish a dancing school. Could he advise her in which neighbourhood to locate such a school? The gentleman replied that the Bloor-Bay shopping district was growing in fashionable importance. "As a matter of fact," he added, "we are coming to Bloor Street now." "Oh! Thank you!" Mother said, suddenly jumping up and abandoning the gentleman. A few minutes later she found an empty brick house one block off Bloor on Bay, and rented it. Two days after our arrival in Canada we were in business.

It was summer as we struggled to get adjusted to Canadian living—*without* servants. My gloomy presentiments with regard to my meals proved justified, for Mother regularly burned the milk and put Ajax instead of salt in the salad. While she was cooking, telephone interruptions made her turn the heat control from high to low and back again so often that weird chemical processes took place in the food. On one occasion some beef turned into a substance resembling chewing-gum. From that time on Daddy took over the kitchen, with ever-increasing improvement in our diet.

My parents, accustomed to cheap labour in the East, had engaged a well known firm to decorate the studio. When the bill came, they almost collapsed. The amount ran into four figures! Realizing that something drastic had to be done, Mother decided to give a show. Up we went to the *Globe & Mail* office, where I sat on the lap of drama critic Herbert Whittaker and showed him my scrapbook. He introduced me in his column as a four-year-old exotic dancer who already had two years' dancing experience. The show featured Mother and her eight pupils, all different ages and proportions. We drew only thirty people in Eaton Auditorium, but almost all became pupils. Of the many dancing schools that have mushroomed in the area since we arrived, ours has become one of the most successful.

By the time I was five, Mother was subjecting me to the discipline of Javanese, Balinese and Hindu dancing. I began to learn "mudras," meaningful Oriental hand movements. I also studied facial expressions depicting "anger," "joy," "sorrow," and "peace." Although the difficult movements taught me muscular control and how to put up with muscle-pain, it was brought out in class that these motions were really unnatural, artificial and disconnected. The different parts of the body did not move in collaboration with each other, but independently from the rest of the anatomy. For instance, the head movements in Oriental dance occur from left to right in quick succession, without influencing the shoulders or the spine. Although this looks rather spectacular and difficult, it is far more difficult to move the head in co-ordination with all the other members of the body. To move the parts of the body in harmony as a single whole is the ideal of free dance.

Mother was said by the newspapers to have "burst upon the Canadian scene with all the effect of a rare tropical bloom." She had done so with her Asiatic dancing. However, her hopes to introduce free dance to the Canadian public went unfulfilled at first, because producers kept typecasting her in Oriental roles. When dance groups all over Canada were invited to submit their compositions for adjudication in the annual Canadian Ballet Festival, Mother ventured to enter a free dance number, together with a Hindu dance arrangement. Since Oriental dance is similar to Western ballet in style, in that they both "disconnect" one part of the body from the others, she easily won one of the twelve available spots with her Hindu work. But the choreography for the free dance piece was rejected. The adjudicator, trained to look for the visual perfection of prescribed body positions, was unprepared either to understand or appreciate free movement. A knowledge of the structure of the body, the various types of locomotion, and the psychological aspects of movement and their relation to one another is essential if one is to appraise natural movement intelligently. This does not mean that free movement cannot be enjoyed intuitively by the layman. It only means that by judging parts of the body separately, one loses track of the movement of the whole, which is the concern of free dance.

But Mother went on with preparing the Hindu work for the festival. At every rehearsal I would become bored just standing around while everyone else danced, so I would jump in unbidden among the others. "Christilot! Go away!" Mother would tell me. I would be gone for a moment. But stubborn as a fly around a sugar bowl, I would be back in my self-appointed place as soon as the dancing began.

Mother gave up in the face of my persistence, deciding that at least she would keep me out of the final rehearsals. But perhaps she unconsciously worked around my improvisations. One day, when she had not brought me to the theatre to practise, she and her fellow dancers found that something was lacking. The dance included a river scene. When Mother came to realize that no Oriental river scene is complete without a child playing about in it, my self-made role was assured.

Of the performance Herbert Whittaker said: "A further distraction was the appearance of Christilot Hanson, a tiny grave exotic who was the cynosure of all eyes as she executed the graceful measures of her dance." Mentioning a group of "personalities that remain in the mind," he honoured me by listing me among them.

The work in the Canadian Ballet Festival led to our being approached shortly afterwards by the National Film Board to do a programme in the series *On the Spot*. I remember how exhausted Mother was, working three days in a row, doing the speaking, drumming and dancing for the show. As for me, I thoroughly enjoyed my part in it, but most of all I enjoyed the upheaval it brought to our home life: meals on the staircase, people discussing the next day's schedule and forgetting to send me to bed, the disorder of cameras, cables and lighting equipment all over the place. I pretended I was a horse and jumped over obstacles. I had never seen a horse other than in story and picture books, yet the idea of riding has been with me ever since I can remember. A painter who was a pupil of Mother's still recalls how at that time I used to follow him around with paper and pencil, forever begging him to draw a horse for me.

The following year brought our biggest assignment to date, when we were invited to dance as guest artists at the Toronto Symphony Promenade Concerts at Varsity Stadium. This was the first time that we would be accompanied by an orchestra. Until now we had always danced to piano accompaniment. In addition, the programme, done to Mother's favourite composer, Tschaikovsky, would be televised.

The *Telegram, Globe & Mail*, and *Star* could not get over the 2,600 persons, the season's largest Prom audience, who turned out at Varsity Stadium. As a result we were engaged for a return performance. This time 3,000 people flocked to the concert, instead of the customary six to eight hundred. Always attracting record crowds, we were the only guest artists to perform twice per season for the following three years, until the Promenade Concerts were discontinued.

The critics praised two works that Mother had choreographed on Canadian themes: "Maria Chapdelaine" and "The Loon's Necklace." I danced the role of Alma Rose in the first and that of an Indian child in the second. With Mother dancing Maria, it was easy for me to interpret Alma Rose. For although the choreography was "set" for the sake of inexperienced members of the company, on the night of the performance Mother always improvised, dancing as her imagination moved her. It was an exhilarating experience to feel transformed into another character and move in a complete other-world under the warm, coloured lights.

Very often we would create entirely new movements. At such times the reactions of the public could certainly be strange! For instance, at the general rehearsal for "The Loon's Necklace" at the Stadium, with Dr. Frieder Weissmann conducting, Mother was upset because she could not recognize the music. It was the same music as had been agreed upon, but the manner in which Dr. Weissmann conducted the composition was so powerful that Mother felt the movements she had choreographed to a piano accompaniment were too small. At the last minute I heard her beg Dr. Weissmann to leave some difficult passages out. He refused, however, because he did not want to confuse his musicians.

Nervously we positioned ourselves in the form of the live totem pole with which our dance began. Despite her apprehension, Mother gave a wonderful interpretation of the old man, Kelora, who was blind but received his sight after having dipped himself into the water with the loon. After the performance was over, she thanked Dr. Weissmann for being so kind as to have omitted the difficult passages anyway. He replied that he hadn't omitted them. "You didn't?" Mother exclaimed, sounding a bit stupid. At that moment people started coming backstage to congratulate her. A blind man was led up to her by a young girl. The girl helped him find Mother's hand, and pressing it fervently, he said, "I *saw* the dance!" A few minutes later Mother asked a friend how she had liked the music composed by Calvin Jackson. "The music?" the friend repeated, just as surprised as Mother had sounded at Dr. Weissmann's answer. "The music? I didn't hear it!"

Puzzled, I asked Mother how the blind man could *see* the dance, while people who weren't deaf did not hear the music! Mother explained to me that the real perception of movement is not visual, but spiritual. One does not "see" movement, one *experiences* it. Since Calvin Jackson's music was specially composed for Mother's choreography and one with it, the blind man, through the vibrations of the tones reaching his ears, *felt* the movements and saw them with an inner vision. And the people who actually saw the dance were only aware of their feelings, which made them unconscious of the sounds reaching their ears.

When I was eight, Mother made me a member of her company and took me on tour with her to the north country. Our professional life became busier and busier. I remember how, after appearing on the programme *Scope* on television, we were flown by jet to Winnipeg at 2:30 a.m. to catch the train to Kenora. There we opened our tour the following day, dancing in tropical sarongs on a cold high school stage.

During these years I went to Branksome Hall in Toronto for my academic studies. Not wanting me to inherit her Javanese accent, Mother also enrolled me in a drama school to learn elocution. One day, CBC-TV phoned up in search of a young girl with dark hair to play the role of an Indian princess in *Howdy-Doody*. I was invited to audition with Basil Coleman, the producer, at Channel 6 studios. When I arrived, candidates ranging in age from the early teens to mid-twenties sat waiting in the producer's room. All that the girls interested in the part had to do was shake hands with a white boy. When it came my turn, I walked up to the boy, silently looked him up and down and, finally reassured, slowly offered him my hand. I won out and was booked for a year on the series.

I earned $50 per show. When my parents told me that they were saving my money to spend it on the thing I would like to have most, I shocked them. I said I wanted a horse.

"A horse!" Mother exclaimed. "Why! You've been looking at too many Westerns."

I could only say, "I've always wanted a horse."

"Well, you can have your horse when you earn first class honours with your piano playing," said Daddy, stalling for time. He knew very well that although I adored music, I disliked practising every day. But soon the piano was plunking away and school work was being thoroughly if mechanically completed, as all my thoughts focused on buying a horse.

Results were noticeable immediately. Whereas previously I had passed my examinations at the Royal Conservatory of Music with 70 per cent, I began to pass them with 80 per cent, the minimum for first class honours. I must say that I was fortunate in having a great teacher, the harpsichordist Greta Krauss. At Branksome Hall my Easter report showed improved marks also. I sang in the school choir, won three piano awards at the Kiwanis Music Festival playing Beethoven, Mozart and Bach, became Junior Sports Day Champion and wrote, produced and directed a school play.

When I promised Mother and Dad that I would maintain this pace, there was little they could do but keep their part of the bargain. After all, I was in a position to buy a horse myself. Every time I went to bed at night, I dreamt about that noblest of animals, and especially about the one that would soon be mine!

2 The horses in my life

"A horse! a horse! my kingdom for a horse!" And a horse I got. "At last maybe we'll get horses out of our system," Mother said with a sigh, as she gave in to the inevitable.

A year had elapsed, during which we had moved from above our Bay-Bloor studio into the country, about twenty miles north of Toronto. I was nine now. My parents had built a split-level bungalow on a two-acre property in Oak Ridges that overlooked a beautiful big pond, where I swam and canoed. I had become a member of the Toronto and North York Pony Club and I spent all my Saturdays there. I attended lectures, learned all I could about grooming, bandaging and first aid, and collected more and more books on horses.

On our street lived a farmer who had two Clydesdales in his backyard. They were kept in a shed. Every day he put their harness on and took them out to the field, where he hitched them up to plow. And every day I was on the look-out for him, clutching two pieces of sugar in my hand. The "clip-clop, jingle-jingle" announcing his approach would bring an ecstatic light to my eyes. Outside our house he would always stop for me to approach my friends. A grateful

18

nod from the big heads and my gift would be eagerly slob-
bered up, leaving my palm delightfully wet.

An observant passerby might have noticed a pair of eyes
peeking from behind a curtain, keeping a discreet but very
attentive vigil over the developing friendship. Since those
days, there have been moments when Mother wished she had
done more than stand silently by. Maybe if she had grabbed
my pony-tail as it fluttered past. . . . But since "all children go
through the horsey phase," she had hoped until the last moment, as other mothers do in such cases, that I would outgrow
my passion for horses.

However, the dreams that a child alone can dream came
true, one by one. I remember how I explored the whole
territory around and about our home. I always played a
horse, one day a black stallion (prompted by the book of the
same name that I had just read), the next a golden palomino.
But regardless of the horse's colour, we, the horse and I (I
acted a dual role), would race across country, up hill and
down dale, until exhausted. Then I'd plump down on a
stump or stone to contemplate a future filled, of course, with
horses.

Today, every time I ride through the bush behind our
house, I get a warm, satisfied feeling from having fulfilled
what was once a fantastic dream. Although I knew nothing at
first about good and bad horse country, now I realize that this
land, with its sandy soil, brush and hills galore, was made for
horses. By some whim of fortune I had been dropped right in
the midst of some of Canada's best horse country. The area
north of Toronto, around Aurora and King, is very heavily
populated with horses and horse people. Our house was only
five minutes by car from the Toronto and North York Hunt
Club and the North York Pony Club headquarters.

How well I remember when Daddy and I drove up to a farm to inspect a horse that was for sale. Neither of us knew anything about horses, except perhaps that they should have four legs and a head. When we arrived in the evening, a groom led us to a box stall from which two bright eyes watched us inquisitively.

The groom went in and made a move to get hold of the horse's halter. "Duffy," a purebred hackney, drew back quickly, as if afraid of the man's hand. The black gelding was headshy. But we did not understand the full meaning of this until Duffy had been bought and transferred to his new home.

Leading the 15-hand horse out of the stall, the groom turned him out in the paddock. There he gave us a good exhibition of his ability to buck, squeal and pigroot. I decided I wanted him! Father, also not in the least disturbed, declared: "He's not sick anyway!" and that was that.

Dad was right. Duffy never had a sick day in his life, and thank goodness for small mercies, because he had enough other idiosyncracies.

Duffy was bought on the rather inauspicious condition that I ride him only under the supervision of a teacher for the first year. His former owner, a lawyer and member of the Toronto and North York Hunt, made no bones about the fact that Duffy had "tricks." But a veterinarian connected with the Pony Club thought I was a match for him.

Arriving for my first ride with Duffy, I grinned from ear to ear, impervious to the startled and amused glances from the more experienced riders. My five-year-old snorted a good bit of fire, prancing around the ring. I was jostled and bounced about the saddle and almost lost my balance, though not my enthusiasm.

"I don't know how the little pumpkin stays on," one horrified man commented to his wife. For Duffy was not exactly a child's horse. But ignorance is bliss, and one could easily pick out my parents, who beamed proudly at the wild performance being given by their daughter. It was more a result of luck than skill that I did not meet with an early accident.

Under the patient guidance of Mr. Robert Hollingsworth, I received a sound education in the basic principles of horsemanship during my first year at the Pony Club. Mr. Hollingsworth's theories were the best foundation I could have had for a positive outlook towards horses. He approached horses in a manner that brings to mind the old saying: "There is something about the outside of a horse that is good for the inside of a man." No question was ever too trivial; from Mr. Hollingsworth I could always expect an answer. Hours were spent discussing and demonstrating the uses of different bridles, and how to clean them. We also passed many happy mornings taking part in quiz games in which the name of every piece of leather had to be known. The same game was played with horses. A horse would be led out on the floor of the barn. Then we would proceed to name every part of his anatomy from his ears down to his fetlocks. Often a local veterinarian gave his time to come and lecture to us on various subjects from proper feeding techniques to first-aid knowledge. I did not find these subjects boring in the least. On the contrary, I found myself constantly delving deeper into the mysteries of "whole" oats versus "rolled" or "crimped" oats.

As for Duffy, he was a cunning animal, wise to all the tricks of the trade. Having a definite opinion about whom he did and did not like, it was common practice for him to be a paragon of virtue as some visitor scrambled awkwardly up into the saddle, and just when security had been attained, boom! the visitor was sitting on the ground, and Duffy was standing in the same position as though nothing had happened.

Another favourite manoeuvre of Duffy's was to stand mutely still in response to leg pressure urging him to move forward. But the moment the legs came off to give a swift kick, he would jerk forward in perfect timing, leaving his victim sprawled behind him in the dirt. Many times I was unhorsed in the sand ring at home during my first months of riding. Undeterred, I'd clamber back aboard until I finally became mistress of Duffy. There was, however, one unalterable flaw in this "mastery." Whenever corn (a grand passion with him) was sighted in a field he'd let out a squeal and I would inevitably be unhorsed in the charge to indulge in this epicurean delight.

But I didn't devote all my time to Duffy. Always attracted by the prospect of new knowledge and challenges, I used to frequent the race track on Saturday mornings. It was early spring, and although Woodbine was full of horses being trained, the races had not yet started. At 6:30 a.m. Daddy would drop me off at the corner of the King Sideroad and Highway 27. There I was picked up by a friend of ours who owned a lead pony and was also an assistant starter. It was not long before I was on friendly terms with some of the trainers.

Without my parents' knowledge I began cooling out thoroughbreds after their morning work-outs. Sometimes I'd be allowed to jog them around the track. It was here that I started to develop a feeling for the gaits and temperaments of different horses. I started to think before I did anything with them, for experience taught me that one careless bump in the saddle, or an accidental kick in the ribs of a sensitive horse, could land me on a fence or in a ditch rather quickly. But during those mornings thoroughbreds won the foremost spot in my heart. Only a few years later could I bring myself to appreciate some of the other breeds of horses.

At dinner one evening, I let the cat out of the bag. As usual I had been giving an account of the exploits of the day when I happened to say that a certain thoroughbred stallion had taken my fancy because his gaits were so smooth. Daddy, whose tone of voice said, "I knew it all the time," asked me how I could know whether his gaits were soft or hard without having ridden him. Because of my hemming and hawing, the situation was as plain as day. After a short lecture on the evil of doing things without the permission of one's parents, the smoke cleared. But Woodbine was ruled out of bounds for twelve-year-old jockeys.

As I diligently absorbed all I could about horses, it became apparent that Duffy was gradually being outgrown. "Gazelle" was purchased for reasons her name implies—speed and jumping ability. Some people said the mare was more Arabian than thoroughbred, others said the opposite. And there was still room for speculation as to whether one or two other strains might be mixed in.

Astride Gazelle, one had the impression of being poised at the top of a ski jump, ready to plummet down to the earth below: her hindquarters stood considerably higher than her forehand. This, however, did not in the least affect my pleasure in riding her. We not only hunted, but experimented on our own. I practised riding bareback, with and without bridle, and even tried riding standing up. When the weather turned hot, I took her for a swim in Lake Wilcox, with just a hackamore. She loved the water, and my only concern was to make sure that she did not go too far. It was very slippery once the water came up, and I had to hold on to her mane not to be left behind. It was this sort of joy in the sport that quieted the nervous little mare into a regular, reliable playmate.

But, like all playmates, we did have our arguments. If I became too daring, or she just decided she had had enough games for the day, she would suddenly stop whatever we were doing to let her head disappear between her knees, and I would be left sitting in front of her, still holding the reins. She never ran off, however. After an outburst of indignant threats, all delivered to her from the ground, I would climb on meekly and take her home. I learned my lesson.

At the hunt Gazelle exhibited remarkable endurance, being able to carry me from morning to night without undue strain. "I can still remember," recalls ex-Master of Foxhounds Robert Elder, "being out on cold, dreary days and repeatedly finding you and your mare, no gloves, frozen cold, and as happy as could be. . . ."

More than once the Toronto and North York Hunt returned on cold late fall afternoons with Colonel Sifton or Robert Elder, Master; Fred Pickford, Huntsman; and me, Field. One afternoon the Huntsman found himself confronted with a very large natural stone jump in his way. Shortly after clearing it he heard a little "plop" behind him and when he looked back, there was I on Gazelle. "You know," Mrs. Pickford told Mother, "my husband was quite impressed with that little mare."

When she asked me about it later, I explained to Mother: "Colonel Sifton said not to push the mare and to go home. But since I didn't know where we were, I had to go on. So I aimed Gazelle at the jump . . . pressed . . . and closed my eyes." In this manner, we did not miss too many hunts that whole year. Hunts were held twice weekly at the Toronto and North York Hunt Club, on Wednesdays and Saturdays. If the meet was to start at the Hunt Club at 7 a.m., I would have to be up at 5 a.m. to feed Gazelle. Since a horse cannot be asked to work on a full stomach, plenty of time is needed to allow for digestion. I would usually give her a hearty breakfast and groom her while she was digesting her food, then run back to the house to have breakfast myself and change into hunting attire.

Six o'clock would find me back in the barn. The tack, consisting of the plain snaffle bridle and English saddle, was quickly put in place and we were ready to go. The time would be exactly 6:15. I had three quarters of an hour to reach the Hunt Club. There was never a soul stirring as we walked and jogged along the concession roads. Only a stray dog would look up guiltily as we passed him raiding someone's garbage cans.

As we approached the Hunt Club, the barking of excited hounds could be heard, mingled with the voices of men shouting orders. Through the mist, one could pick out horses and horse-trailers parked here and there. Greys, blacks, chestnuts, browns, all were being walked around, their lithe muscles flexing, their eyes eager, their flanks quivering slightly for the start that was not far off.

Soon the cry " 'Ware hounds!" was up. The kennel doors were flung open and a stream of black, tan and white hounds spilled out onto the field. They grouped around the Huntsman, waiting for the signal to start off.

The Master glanced at his watch. It read 7 a.m. exactly. The hunt began. The Huntsman and the hounds led the procession and the Master followed, with the field spread out behind him. Nervous horses fidgeted as they headed down the back of the club and into the woods. Then the pace settled down to a good jog, everyone trying to keep in line and not run up too close to the horse in front.

" 'Ware hole!" came the cry from the front, and was echoed all the way down the line. As one rode by, a big gopher hole could be seen right on the path. A horse could easily break a leg if he stepped in it. The pace slowed down to a walk while, one by one, the horses jumped the log pile that barred their way. Usually there was no problem getting the horses over obstacles, since no horse wants to be left behind after seeing his neighbour go over.

We were now in the field, waiting while the hounds did their work in the covert. No talking was allowed, since it would distract the hounds, but the Huntsman shouted encouragement to them. Suddenly a few hounds started to "give tongue." The others immediately ran to them, and all together they broke across the field, the Huntsman with them.

The mad dash was on. Horses and hounds charged through the tangled woods, over coops and stone walls, down ravines and up the banks of streams. Dirt and mud from churning hooves filled the air but no breach of etiquette was committed should a gentleman's horse smear a lady. The fast horse led, whether lady's or gentleman's.

Suddenly the Master held up his hand, the signal for the field to come to a stop. We waited once more while Huntsman and hounds could be heard thrashing around in the woods, trying to pick up the scent. And so the day passed. The scent was found and then lost again, but whether in the end the hounds made their kill, or sly "Reynard" escaped, it made little difference to me. The thrill of the gallops, the chance to see nature close up, those were my reasons for hunting.

Finally the Master would decide that we had all had enough sport for the day, and we would turn homeward. The horses would no longer be eager to prance and dance. They would walk quietly on loose reins, while their riders also sat back and relaxed, and recounted the number of fences jumped that day, or the number of close calls.

Visions of coffee and eggs floated in my head as I neared home, and I liked to believe that Gazelle also was thinking of the warm bran mash she knew was a ritual on hunt nights. That night I was sure I would sleep soundly, images flickering through my head as on a slide projector: Gazelle jumping over the ditch, Gazelle over the wall, Gazelle side-stepping the groundhog hole I had not even seen!

On February 19, 1960, I received a letter signed by Lady Eaton, Honorary Life Master of the Toronto and North York Hunt, and Colonel Clifford Sifton and Mr. Robert Elder, Joint Masters. "We take pleasure," the letter began, "in inviting you to join the select band of accomplished Foxhunters authorized to wear the colours of the Toronto and North York Hunt and to maintain and carry forward the activities and sporting traditions of this ancient and attractive pastime. It is our privilege to present to you herewith your first set of Hunt Buttons and Blue Flannel Collar."

I was thrilled when the honour I had secretly dreamed about was so suddenly bestowed upon me. I was grateful to have had the opportunity to hunt with such a highly esteemed group and will always be proud to wear their colours.

By this time I was getting ready to move up to another horse. In horse shows and hunter trials Gazelle performed well. But many times we were called to line up first or second, only to be shuttled to the back when bigger competitors were placed ahead, by virtue of their more classic conformation. In the hunt field, where a horse is judged on his performance, Gazelle's down slant was overlooked, as everyone knew the reliability, jump and speed of the mare. Still, the fact remained that she was not easy to ride.

When, therefore, a woman approached me to buy Gazelle, it was my turn to have some misgivings, although the lady in question had a few years' hunting experience. She was a good sport, however, and quite daring, and did not hold it against me that she broke her foot soon after she began to ride Gazelle.

Once they both fell into a snow drift at the Hunt Club. Gazelle was the quicker scrambler and made straight off towards her old barn. From the determined pace at which she trotted off, Gazelle's new owner had an idea of where she was going. She drove her car to our place. And sure enough, standing with a drooping head in front of her old stall was Gazelle, melted snow dripping from her disheveled mane, and steam rising from her flanks. But time and patience finally adjusted Gazelle to her new home, and the following fall she carried her owner to the winning of her hunt colours.

Although it was a painful parting, I realized that I could not keep each horse I owned forever. Sam Jarvis, a thoroughbred breeder of considerable renown, agreed to help me in my quest for a better-looking horse. Sam, after whose family Jarvis Street is named, still remembers the time when he had to hack his horse all the way to the Royal Winter Fair to show. And in his opinion there was only one kind of horse that would meet my demands: a thoroughbred.

Wandering through the barns at Woodbine with my

parents, I saw many horses. And the more we saw, the more Mother disliked the idea of a "showy" horse. During one of these excursions, while talking to an assistant trainer, I informed him I thought one of his young mares was sick. "Oh really now," he said in a condescending tone of voice. "Let's go and see." He examined the horse quickly. "No, there's nothing wrong with her." That happened early in the afternoon. Late that night the trainer, seeing a light burning in our home, drove in. It seemed the horse had become quite sick in the evening and he wished to find out how I had known.

"I'll ask her," Mother said. "Chris. . . Chris. . ." she whispered, gently shaking me awake. "How did you know that the mare was sick this afternoon?"

"I saw it in her eyes," I mumbled from beneath the covers.

Phoning us the next evening, Sam said he had a prospect for me to look at. He thoughtfully suggested that I come alone. The horse belonged to Brian Herbinson, a member of Canada's bronze medal three-day event team in 1956. Sam informed Brian he had a buyer, and a date was set. Brian planned to hack the horse over to Sam's place, where I could try him.

All morning Brian brushed and cleaned his brown colt, even plaiting the mane for the afternoon's demonstration. Then he set out to meet me at Sam's on "Colonel W's" back. Sam was waiting at the appointed time. I don't know just what went through Brian's mind at the sight of the prospective buyer, who turned out to be a little Pony Clubber he knew quite well!

Colonel W had been purchased straight from the track for Brian's wife. But she could not ride him every day and he had become too much of a handful. Brian let me mount his four-year-old. We seemed to get along very well from the start and had no difficulty adjusting to each other. Later that evening, seated in the living room, I leaned back and exulted in the afternoon's ride with closed eyes. "Mmmm," I thought, "his gaits are as soft as velvet."

"Eight hundred dollars! There must be something wrong with the horse!" said the incredulous instructor, a former international rider, as he admired my lovely thoroughbred. He motioned to me to mount.

For my first lesson on a quality horse, I warmed up Bonheur (for so I had named him) on large circles, being careful to leave his mouth alone and not ask him to do anything that I felt would upset him. But as the lesson progressed, commands that he was not ready to follow were given. The situation became tense. As soon as I gathered the reins and demanded something from him, he fought and pulled and worked himself into a frenzy. Soon the temperamental horse was galloping out of control. There was no time to consider any more what was being screamed at me, and I brought the horse back to a walk, the only way I knew how.

My teacher marched up to me and asked me to dismount. Bonheur was fidgeting nervously with his head. I hoped that he would behave, thereby saving himself the punishment that would otherwise come his way. My instructor mounted. Desperate, I watched with a troubled heart. A short but violent battle followed.

"You have spoiled him already," I was told, while being handed the reins of the heavily lathered horse. "You have let him get away with murder!"

I could not help bursting into tears, although I am not given to crying much, especially before spectators. I felt hopeless and humiliated, but above all I cried for Bonheur. I could not stand the tormented look in his eyes, the wildness that was caused by fear, driving him to run anywhere, into anything. The horse named "happiness" was unrideable for weeks.

As Mother watched me daily walking the trembling, absolutely unmountable animal, she began to wonder whether we had bought a "crazy" horse. Finally I managed to get on his back, speaking soothing words and being careful not to touch his sides. But Bonheur was unpredictable. He would walk one moment, and the next he would be two fields away, before I had time to gather up the reins. When I turned up at the Pony Club with him, the gloomy predictions started. "He's too much for her!" "He's mad!" "Fancy buying a horse like that for a Pony Clubber!" "She won't be ready to ride him for another three years!"

Amused, I told Mother about some of the remarks. One evening a member of the Hunt Club expressed the opinion that Bonheur would be my "grave" some day. Mother was far from amused, however. Everyone was prophesying disaster and she was beginning to get frantic. She didn't know whom to turn to for sound advice concerning this horse that she wished she had never seen.

My tears and pleading saved Bonheur from being sold immediately. He was allowed to stay under the condition that he be ridden only under the supervision of a teacher. But every lesson ended in upsets and tears.

In her concern to dispose of the horse, Mother did not fully appreciate the mutual bond that was developing between Bonheur and me. Left alone, we would go along fine. But as soon as someone came to teach me and I started following commands, Bonheur resorted to senseless running.

Once he did that, I was not strong enough to pull him up and just had to sit there, guiding him in ever smaller circles until he stopped of his own accord.

Yet he showed his affection for me by being very jealous. He always stationed himself between me and other horses and he was furious with any attention I gave to any creature but himself. It is interesting to realize that he is the only horse I have never fallen off! Somehow other people managed to get hurt now and then when working around him. (One girl who helped me in a Pony Club rally was knocked out by his nodding head.) But I have a feeling that he always protected me, even though I had to be careful.

A repeat performance with another instructor and things were not looking very happy at all. "Maybe she really has spoiled the horse," Mother thought. For weeks again Bonheur was a nervous wreck. But I did my best to be as gentle and patient as possible with him until he became calm once more. I shampooed his tail with expensive lotions and constantly rubbed his coat to a brilliant sheen, and Bonheur responded to this attention with a loyalty that has never diminished.

With the experts predicting disaster and me happy as I had never been before, Mother continued in her turmoil. Seeking the right answer, she stumbled upon the name of a certain General von Oppeln Bronikowski who was visiting near Oak Ridges. A newspaper article noted that the General had been a member of the German dressage team that had won the gold medal in the 1936 Berlin Olympics.

Having graduated from a Viennese school, Mother knew about the famous Spanish Riding School in Vienna and about dressage, the art of riding that gives one such a firm seat that it is impossible for any horse to get rid of his rider.

On an impulse, Mother phoned the General and explained our situation to him. He kindly consented to come and have a look at Bonheur.

"If the horse won't go for him either," Mother announced, "then you have really spoiled him!"

The judgment day came and the General arrived, dressed in immaculate black. Fearing the worst, I led out my dearest companion. I showed Bonheur first without saddle, so that the General could have a good look at his conformation and type. He turned to Mother, and said in German, "Do you know that I have never possessed such a beautiful horse in my life." Feeling that we had passed the first part of the examination, I saddled Bonheur up for the final verdict.

The General mounted with *élan* and moved off. I prayed with an expressionless face that did not betray the feelings welling up from within. At least Bonheur was moving forward and not backwards as he had done under other teachers. The General's stern face became softer. Finally a smile broke out as he enjoyed the comfortable gaits of my young mount. Bonheur was tactfully being given his head by the General's wise hands.

After a short while the General dismounted and asked to see me ride. With a joyful heart I mounted and rode off. Bonheur responded to my feelings of elation and went better than ever before.

"She is worth teaching," the General said to Mother.

"Will you teach her?" Mother returned in his language.

"On Sundays, that is the only time I am free."

That night I began my studies in German. The General did not speak English.

 *Anatole*

Bonheur and I had scarcely begun our training with the General when, much to our regret, he had to return to Germany for the winter. When he came back to Canada, his obligations were such that I was unable to receive further training from him. But in that summer of 1961 when I found myself without a teacher, Anatole Pieregorodzki had just founded the Canadian Olympic Equestrian Centre at Newmarket. If it had not been for Anatole, I would never have reached Tokyo!

Anatole Pieregorodzki, author of *A Guide for the Combined Training of the Horse,* was the most exuberantly dedicated man I have ever met. Not a dominating figure, his light, wiry frame possessed an immense energy and agility. What struck me most about him were his clear blue eyes. They had a quick, intense quality, especially when he was explaining something about horses.

Born in Poland, Anatole had been a major in the Polish Armoured Division during the Second World War. He had come to Canada in 1949, and by 1952 had an Olympic three-day event team ready to represent Canada for the first time. From then on he kept coaching the Canadian Olympic

Equestrian Team, which rode to a bronze medal in Stockholm in 1956 and a gold at the Pan American Games in Chicago three years later. When Anatole and I had known each other for a little while, he decided that his goal for me was the Grand Prix de Dressage at the 1964 Tokyo Olympics.

How often Anatole's confidence was to support me through an ordeal, when the doubt and hopelessness every athlete has to go through threatened to get me down! What he loved most, I believe, was the sheer beauty of the horse in motion. Once I was standing with the Major at the paddock gate, while Bonheur was turned out to exercise and enjoy the sunshine. Suddenly a horse appeared two fields away, galloping towards the stable. Bonheur's head came up, he stood alert and quivered with excitement. His tail stiffened out and his nostrils widened. The Major turned to me, his eyes bright with sudden emotion. "This is the horse as I love him, alive, eager, and free!" Then Bonheur raced down the field to greet the newcomer. At that moment I felt that I had learned a new truth, that I had witnessed an approach to life to be emulated: living joyous and free of tension is the lesson to be learned from a spirited horse.

At the time of our enrolment with Anatole, Bonheur and I had no idea what was awaiting us. "The Centre" was only twelve miles from home, but my horse had to put up with my terrible nerves the day I packed him in cotton and put his bandages on, to drive him to Newmarket. After a too lengthy preparation, he walked into the old horse trailer with no trouble and stood contentedly munching hay while father and daughter loaded saddle, bridles, brushes and all the other miscellaneous articles which no horse travels without, into the car. At last the engine started up and we drove very slowly out of our driveway.

By now Daddy was used to the nervous creature beside him who at intervals screamed: "Don't go too fast!" "Be careful!" or sat silently brooding about the dangers of vanning horses. Nevertheless, we had always arrived safe and sound before, and this time was no exception. At the Centre, I unloaded Bonheur and walked him around a bit to get him used to his new environment. Then I chose a big, roomy box stall for him in the barn, which gradually filled to capacity during the next few days.

Activities at the Training Centre revolved entirely around Anatole, or "Tolley," as we sometimes called him. He led us in more ways than one. A silent battle started among the pupils and their teacher as to who could come up with the craziest sun hat. Anatole's entry was a white baseball cap, with a ridiculously long visor to keep the sun's glare off his face. My choice was a straw tyrolean-shaped affair, with an orange chain around the brim and a large, multi-coloured straw flower sitting off centre. One enterprising boy cut the top out of his hat and went around sporting the brim only! The result was that all could be identified from a distance.

Horse people are never considered quite normal by normal people. After all, who would get a kick out of sitting on an uncomfortable 1500 pounds of moving tyranny? It takes a certain type of character. One can, of course, imagine the consequences when a dozen or so of these individuals are thrown together to take part in a course. The high jinks, the kidding and the unrelenting labour combined to make a rare mood in which we all thrived. Gone was the everyday drudgery of life, gone were our personal fears, and we galloped, jumped and longed, even ate, in a marvellous "do or die" mood.

A typical day started at eight in the morning when everyone groomed his horse and saddled up for the first lesson at nine. We all congregated in the riding ring to wait for the Major. He arrived carrying loads of longeing equipment, consisting of pairs of side reins, longe lines and longeing whips. Soon the ring settled down to quiet serious work, with horses circling around, their owners in different corners of the ring. Anatole moved from one to the other, giving a tip about the way to hold a whip, or extricating some poor girl from the coils of rope in which she had become entangled.

We then proceeded to mounted work, everyone practising the exercises the Major had laid down for us. In my case, "exercises" meant trotting in figure eights, sometimes for half an hour, to relax Bonheur and teach him to flex around my inside leg. The same exercises at the canter followed, in which I had to make sure to change leads correctly every time we changed direction. The lesson ended by schooling over some *cavalletti* (cavalletto, cavalletti in the plural, is the Italian word for "little horse"), rails that are supported by small wooden blocks affixed to each end. Usually six to eight cavalletti rails were spaced at five-foot intervals for horses to trot over. Sometimes small jumps were set up. The emphasis, however, was always on quietness and good form over a fence rather than height.

The horses were then cooled out and returned to their boxes to rest, but alas, the riders had to continue working. Anatole brought out two fresh horses and let a couple of the older boys longe the riders. We mounted in turn, crossed our stirrups over the withers of the horse, and concentrated on sitting in the saddle while the horses trotted around in circles. We were completely at the mercy of the person longeing the horse, a point which was taken advantage of once in a while.

A favourite manoeuvre was to start the horse suddenly before its rider had a chance to settle down in the saddle,
thereby causing a lot of scrambling and clutching at leather
to retain the precarious position. It was done in good fun,
though, and those who bit the dust were never too annoyed.
However, it makes a difference when one is longed in the
right position, which is very hard to describe in words, because it involves the co-ordination of the *whole* body, not just
the buttocks. The muscle-pain which comes from being
longed in the right position is indescribable, as I found out
three years later when a pupil of the Neindorff *Reitinstitut*.
During that summer at the Centre, however, I was still far
from sitting properly, and the longeing did not bother me
much.

A lunch break followed, in which Anatole showed films of
international events or gave lectures on all subjects from
feeding to conditioning a horse for jumping, cross-country or
dressage. In the afternoon the horses were saddled up once
more. Anatole, mounted also, took us across country, showing
us how to go up and down hills correctly, how to regulate our
paces and jump the natural obstacles that were scattered all
over the farm.

Every second or third day Anatole announced cheerfully:
"We are going to gallop today!" He then took us out to a big
hayfield around which a track had been laid. One of us
started galloping around the track and when he was about
700 yards away, the next horse began. All were supposed to
keep the same galloping distance apart, except for ex-race
horses like Bonheur, who considered themselves exceptions.
We started out slowly enough, but it wasn't long before the
wind in our faces and the exhilaration of the galloping
turned Bonheur into a full-fledged runner once more. In no

time I was shrieking helplessly to Anatole that we were out of control. He bellowed instructions through the megaphone: "Don't panic!" After three laps around the track Bonheur slowed down of his own accord. After a few such experiences he was banished from the track, and I had to be content with riding in the ring while the others galloped.

The Junior International Horse Show was the climax of the two-week course. For the older boys it meant a week of hectic last-minute preparations. Besides setting up a show ring and mowing the fifty acres surrounding it, they had to dig water jumps and put portable stalls in the arena for visiting horses.

The stadium jumps were all freshly painted. The jump standards were white, with red, black and blue striped poles between them. Truckloads of freshly cut cedar branches were stuffed into rectangular boxes and neatly clipped across the top, adding colour and variety to the obstacles. The water jump had two plastic ducks floating on the water. Set in the corner of a huge rolling field with one shady tree as its ornament, the beautiful jumping ring delighted spectators. A low stone wall had a figure half prostrated across it. A grisly face that probably would have frightened a bear, as it did a couple of horses, smiled out from above a neck that was visibly stuffed with straw. Not one horse knocked a rail off this jump, making sure to keep as far from the grotesque intruder as possible. The finely mowed footing was delightful to horses descending from a five-foot effort, and it set off the whole spectacle with an air of medieval tournament majesty.

This was to be the first junior international horse show in Canada. It brought together the cream of young riders from our country and the United States. General von Oppeln was among the spectators and was again impressed with Bonheur, both on the first day, which consisted of the usual junior events such as equitation classes, and the second day, devoted to the Junior Nations' Cup. Competition for the Cup was divided into one round in the morning and one in the afternoon.

Anatole had chosen Bruce Cuddy, Larry Bowen and me to compete as the Centre's team in the Nations' Cup. In order not to tire the horses for this event, we were to choose only three classes to show in on the first day. I chose two equitation classes and one open jumper class to warm up for the big event. In equitation the riders are judged on their seat and ability to manage their mounts in the basic gaits: walk, trot, and canter. We wound up reserve champions. In the open jumper class Bonheur went splendidly for a green horse, and came third. I bumped into Brian Herbinson, Bonheur's former owner, who declared that Bonheur would have won the class had it been judged as a working hunter class, because he went clean, in style and in an even pace. As it was, two other horses made better time.

The next day, Bruce, Larry and I spent the waiting hours joshing around with each other, trying to keep our jumpy nerves steady. Bruce, over six feet tall, got rubbed about his height continually, but he never wavered, even when someone called out as he sailed over a jump: "Hey Cuddy! Do you want an oxygen mask?" and other suitable comments.

Larry was his usual phlegmatic self and the only one calm enough to smile at every camera that was aimed his way. As far as I was concerned, I am afraid I was so nervous that I messed it up for the team, for although we went well in the morning round, having two knock-downs, we almost came to grief over the huge in-and-out jump. It was a combination obstacle, consisting of two separate fences that were so spaced as to allow the horse only one stride between them. The sight awaiting a horse as he approached the first jump was not encouraging. Wrong timing on the first fence would put him too close to, or too far away from, the second fence to jump it smoothly. Somehow we managed to scramble over the first time. The afternoon was something else again. Bonheur and I came in wrong for the dreaded in-and-out, and refused out.

After the competition was over, Anatole found me walking my horse around to cool him off. And then came the incident that showed me the calibre of Anatole as a man, trainer and psychologist. "Chris, saddle up Bonheur and come to the ring," he told me. "You are going to jump that in-and-out." His friends were waiting for him to join them in the after-show celebrations, yet Anatole dropped everything to insist that the "young horse," as he called Bonheur, be schooled over the jump that had frightened him earlier in the day. "Tomorrow will be too late," he declared. "Now."

I saddled up and rode out to the now deserted ring where only minutes ago hundreds had flocked. Anatole, carrying a hunting whip and lash, followed us out silently. After a few minutes' warm-up he asked me to go at the fence quietly. Bonheur, as was expected, stopped dead.

"O.K." Anatole said. "Now once more and drive!"

I turned for the jump again and as I approached, the whip flew into action, catching Bonheur around the quarters. He laid his ears back and with a surge he was up and over the fence.

"Mission accomplished," said Anatole, smiling. "But try it again for good measure."

This time we sailed over without hesitation and after

jumping a few smaller obstacles to relax we went home, all feeling much happier.

It was Anatole's firm and quiet command of all situations that made riders trust him as they did. I had experienced and learned much in those weeks, and yet I hungered for more. I was immensely grateful when my parents told me I could stay for another course in the fall.

The course had just begun when the Centre was again getting ready for a show. This time it was a one-day event. Anatole himself designed the jumps and set up the flags marking his difficult cross-country fences. As an artist signs his completed canvas, the Major took delight in adding a personal touch to his work. For example, a rider and a horse would come galloping up to the brim of a ravine, housing an obstacle at the bottom, and find a sign greeting them: "Dragon pit! Ha! Ha! Ha!" Many a time these touches of humour inspired the little more courage needed to jump one's horse with confidence, so necessary for successful negotiation.

One day Anatole decided to get his measuring wheel out and walk the course, inspecting jumps on the way. It was a hot, humid day, overcast, with rain threatening. Nevertheless, we started out, Anatole and I and some others. We had walked over three or four acres and were at the farthest corner of the farm. All of a sudden a wind came up, the horizon went black and a severe thunderstorm began. We all started rushing for home. Anatole ran a short way, then, laughing, said that he was wet already and might as well walk. He looked pale. Wet through, we all reached the farm house, where Anatole immediately asked to lie down for a while, as he did not feel well. We left him to rest a bit, not realizing how serious the disturbance was. He had suffered a heart attack.

While we waited for Anatole's recovery, autumn advanced slowly. One evening when General von Oppeln was over at our house for dinner, it was decided to send Bonheur and me to Germany for further training. To my great surprise the General expressed doubts as to whether Bonheur would stand up to the rigorous training for the Grand Prix. In the end his uncertainty affected us all, and we sadly agreed to sell Bonheur. A buyer was found in the United States and a date set on which my horse would be fetched. How I dreaded the day! But once more destiny intervened. At the last moment the American gentleman called to say that business matters prevented him from going through with the deal! I was delighted and relieved that instead of my having to buy a new horse in Europe, Bonheur would be flown over to Hannover, where the General lived, and trained with me. I solemnly vowed to myself that I would never consent to part with him again.

With everything ready at last, and the farewells completed with the usual exhortations to "write," I left Canada for the Continent. I went by boat with the General and his family. Bonheur followed about ten days later by plane.

I had spent almost four months in Germany when I received a letter from Anatole, saying he hoped to be up on horseback at Christmas to conduct a course at the Centre. The Centre was the supreme expression of his devotion to Canadian horsemanship, for he realized that only when horse and rider are fully trained from youth can Canada expect success in international competition. He thought it highly unsatisfactory to rally a team only one year before every Olympiad. Always giving his all, he mounted too early after his sickness, and one day, riding in the arena with his pupils and explaining some technical points, he stopped in the middle of a sentence.

And so Anatole died while teaching and riding at the Centre he had founded. There was no one to take his place. His widow, Irene, sent me an unfinished letter in which he urged me never to give up jumping. That letter and Anatole's dedication and enthusiasm have become my greatest inspirations. As long as I am riding, I don't want to let him down.

4 First trip to Germany

There is a German expression to describe the period of adolescence: *himmelhoch jauchzend, zum Tode betrübt.* It means that the adolescent is inclined to be either in high spirits, when he could "shout sky-high with joy," or in a state of despondency, when he "grieves to death." Whether I was just going through the period of adolescence, or that in comparison with the inspiring summer with Anatole, every other experience had to seem drab, or that for the first time I was far away from home, one thing was certain: my first winter in Hannover was the bleakest time of my life.

The family Schneider, who opened their home to the little foreigner, were very sympathetic and understanding, but no horse people. I could not share my daily riding experiences with them. And the General, although an excellent teacher, treated his pupils "professionally," without sentiment. Thus Bonheur and I were having a hard time of it, since we'd both been utterly spoiled with love before.

On the ship I had felt the separation from my parents deeply. I remember staying on deck after we sailed out of New York harbour, until I could no longer see the North American coastline. As I stared at those huge waves, a strange panic took hold of me, and I wished Mother and Dad were there. I kept reading Mother's letter. I got much comfort from it. As the miles between us increased, I realized I had taken for granted the home I knew and loved so well. I took a good look at myself and my self-appointed task to represent my country in dressage, and I became aware that it was not the riding alone that challenged me, but the courage to bear homesickness and fear. Could I do it?

In Germany, the first impression I made upon Christine, the Schneiders' daughter, was that I was frivolous, because I wore lipstick. Christine was my age, fourteen, and the two of us shared a room. In Germany teenagers are considered children and are supposed to look that way. A girl who puts on the slightest make-up is called "painted." I must say I began to feel more and more conspicuous, and after using lighter and lighter colours, I finally went "natural" too.

Mr. and Mrs. Schneider taught me how to live economically in Germany. On their advice I bicycled every day to where Bonheur was stabled, at the other end of the city. The bus and the "tram" took too long, and the cost was high. That made for an hour's pedalling each day.

My first impression of Hannover was that I might never get out of it alive. Cars went any way they pleased and streetcars stopped barely long enough to allow passengers to leap on and off. Crosswalks, lights, meant nothing. Even on sidewalks I almost got trampled to death by 200-pound ladies who went crashing through everybody and everything.

It was as if the weather kept company with my low spirits. The mist hung unusually gray and dense as I came out of the Schneider home on the Lüneburger Damm, ready for my daily half-hour jaunt to where Bonheur was stabled at the Hannover Race Track. As it was nearing winter, I bundled up well before getting on Christine's bicycle. I had to be at the stables at seven, so as to have Bonheur ready for the General by eight. Not for a moment did I entertain the thought of being late. The General already had me drilled to carry out his slightest command.

Oh! Sometimes the pain of sitting trot! I used to start out with sitting trot, then do extended trot, then again sitting trot, and at first it was agony, but I found that each day things became a bit easier. At the Pony Club in Canada I would have complained loudly and bitterly had I been asked to do sitting trot any longer than a quarter of an hour at a time. However, the exercises helped to give me a securer seat. Then the General dropped my stirrups four holes!

Bonheur also began to feel the effects of the steady, unrelenting work-outs that must have made his former racing days seem like a carefree and too distant youth. To relieve his muscle-aches I massaged his back and legs with litres of rubbing alcohol, and bought cod liver oil for his feed and his feet.

Work increased. Bonheur began losing weight, but I went the other way, being unaccustomed to the German diet that consisted mainly of potatoes and heavy brown bread. The leisure hours at home were spent keeping up my piano studies with a German teacher. These were the bright moments of the day. Mrs. Schneider, who had sacrificed a singing career for her family, often asked me to accompany her as she went through her repertoire of *Lieder*. The lyrics of these songs made me want to acquaint myself with the works of Goethe, Heine and other German poets.

Comparing notes with Christine, I discovered that the standard of learning is higher in Europe than in North America. I often studied in the evenings with some of Christine's friends from the university. My favourite subject was philosophy, especially ancient Greek philosophy, because it portrays ugliness and discord as allied to evil. The value of art in the eyes of the philosophic Greeks lay in its aid to individual development. As such, art was considered a means to the end of good living, not an end in itself. I believe that unless one looks upon the art of one's choice as a means to understanding life, one cannot develop the courage and perseverance necessary to master its particular technique.

It was inspiring for me to learn about one of the outstand-ing horsemen of history, Xenophon, the Athenian general who was also a follower of Socrates. Xenophon's most famous work, I was told, was the *Anabasis*, a story of ordeal and triumph. Ten thousand soldiers, with Xenophon as their com-mander, landed in a desperate situation in enemy territory, only to be told to "show some superiority to misfortune." A natural leader, Xenophon inspired willing rather than forced obedience, and after many trials he and his troops finally succeeded in reaching home. This is also the key to success as a rider. I know that only if one succeeds in persuading one's mount to obey willingly can one expect a spirited yet relaxed performance from him. This principle underlay the physical and psychological control that the ancient Greek rider at-tained over his mount, so that he became a centaur: horse and man in one.

No matter how dark things seemed in the daytime, the Greek ideals which inspired me at night helped me through. For the General was a stern teacher, very miserly in his praise, very liberal in his rebukes. I was glad I did not always understand the words that came flying in my direction. But this much I knew, they were soldierly words, not customarily used towards ladies. Looking back upon the period, I am glad

I was trained as a soldier, having to take screaming and swearing in cold blood.

Speaking of blood, it came through my breeches where I rode myself raw on the insides of my legs. It was a long process every night getting the material little by little off my skin with lukewarm water. I did not dare complain, but once in a while I had a great longing to fly back home; I'd have liked to get out of the relentless day-after-day schedule. Then I would look at my dear horse, who had endured so much without complaining, and be ashamed of my feelings. They came less and less frequently and finally grew out of my system.

As a pianist must first limber up his fingers at the keyboard before he can start playing, so Bonheur and I went through weeks and months of basic, repetitious movements of loosening and suppling, always striving for an even, cadenced rhythm in all our work. On circles, squares, eights, and other figures I would bend my horse into shoulder-ins (haunches out), then into sideways or travers-like (haunches in) movements, until he would bend like rubber.

When he was first taken off the track, Bonheur had been able only to walk and gallop. His trot had been practically non-existent. Under the General, in the summer of 1960, he had first started to walk, trot, and canter on both leads, free, almost without contact and with natural head carriage. The fall of 1961 in Germany was spent on flexing, shoulder-ins, voltes, and ordinary and extended cantering. We did pirouettes in walk, trot, and canter in proper flexion and counterflexion, that is, with the head in the direction the horse was moving and then turned away from the direction of the movement. In the fourth month our progress was more noticeable. The long hours of work were paying off and the actual two-tracks were asked for, only two or three steps at a time . . . then Bonheur would tense. Care was taken to strengthen the hind legs for the added weight they would have to bear as the degree of collection became higher.

Sunday was the one day of rest for Bonheur, therefore Monday was always my worst day for riding. My thorough-bred had all sorts of stable fire and he really put on a show. He bucked as I never imagined he would, and I never came closer to being thrown than during those days. When the General screamed "Pu-ush!" and I drove Bonheur forward, he stubbornly refused to go, and when I hit him with the crop, he stood on his hind legs.

Next, work on the flying changes began. All other work was discontinued for weeks while we concentrated solely on achieving the flying change. In the beginning it was one of the hardest lessons to learn. At first the changes just wouldn't go, and each day would come and go and we still had not mastered it. Depression settled on me, on Bonheur, and on the General. At one point I had to fight with myself regularly to keep my enthusiasm up. It was such a long, hard struggle. But I knew that if I could not overcome discouragement in riding, I would have to conquer myself in some other direc-tion. Then one day when I gave him the aid, Bonheur changed leads, as easily as anything! The joy I felt at that moment was indescribable. So I learned to take failure and defeat until victory came.

Eventually I mastered flying changes at the middle of a figure eight, on the diagonal, and finally on the long side of the arena up to every fourth stride. Then work on this special movement ceased and the horse returned to trot exercises, with ever-increasing engagement of the hindquarters. Hours were spent refining lessons already learned.

In the spring, my parents had to interrupt my European training, since the costs were mounting so high. But before I was scheduled to return to Canada in June, Mother wrote to the General and asked him to enter me in a German horse show to give me European competition experience. If she had hidden a bomb in the letter, the General could not have exploded more. However, spluttering and muttering, he grumpily complied with the request, stressing in a letter to Mother that it was *her* idea, not his. In contrast to Anatole, who seemed to possess boundless optimism, the General was always saying that "things just cannot be achieved between today and tomorrow."

I was entered in the *Pferdeleistungsschau* in Gehrden on May 25 and 26. At this time I was fifteen years old. Although it was a national horse show, I received special permission from the organizers to take part in the competition, in order to "show Canada Germany's co-operation towards a sporting colleague," and also to "meet with the personal wishes of the General."

Fearing that his young charge would be overwhelmed by her sixty-six adult competitors, the General made his entrance on the big day from the far side of the show grounds. I do not know what went through his head when I came out the victor. The prize money had to go to a German, so I received a trophy and a bouquet of roses. The next day the General did not mind being associated with me and Bonheur. He warmed the horse up at the show grounds and helped me prepare for the test. There were thirty-three competitors in the harder test and I placed third. I was so happy I had not let my teacher down!

The General wrote to my parents that he was amazed at the progress we had made in such a short time. He attributed our success to the combination of horse and rider, which he called, "without exaggeration a quite rare and happy coincidence." He insisted that a case like this would scarcely ever be repeated. He was of the opinion that I was a "natural" and had a passion for riding, but that without Bonheur it would have been impossible for me to have registered the successes I had at my age.

Whatever the theory of it all, I was grateful, tired, and happy to go home! I put away the written critiques of the German judges who had praised Bonheur for his *"leichtes, flüssiges galoppieren* (easy, fluid canter) ." In both tests remarks were made upon the "harmony between rider and horse," his "beautiful, straight entrance," "good voltes," "correct halts," "supple backing-up," and "collected canter with much impulsion," all of which proved that we had been given a good foundation in dressage.

By German standards Bonheur was now an "M" (*medium*) dressage horse. The first stage is "L" (*leicht*), meaning "easy," in Canada equal to the elementary level. The horse at "M" level has to be able to do all sideways movements (shoulder-in, travers, renvers), the two-track movements in trot and canter, and pirouettes. However, Bonheur could do one movement that actually belongs in the "S" (*schwer*) class, meaning "difficult": the flying change every second stride. An "S" horse is of Grand Prix level, the level demanded of a horse in the Olympics.

On June 27, Bonheur and I left Europe on a KLM freighter, landing in Montreal where Daddy met us with our old trailer to drive us home. I realized that the months in Europe had been good for me, and that I couldn't have stood it alone, without Bonheur. The knowledge that he needed me and I needed him helped us to continue our work.

I arrived home in time to take part in the Second Junior International at the Centre. Bonheur and I won two medals in the Equitation and Equitation over Jumps classes, introducing the flying change for the first time in a Junior show. But it wasn't the same without Anatole. I am sure I was not the only one who missed him.

In October of the same year, Bonheur and I competed in our first international dressage test, the Prix St. Georges, at Washington, D. C. The judges were the late Major-General N. F. Leschly from Copenhagen; Commandant J. S. Paillard from Paris; and Colonel D. W. Thackeray, from the United States. The Prix St. Georges is the third-hardest international test. We came second, two points behind the 1960 Olympic dressage representative of the United States. And in November, as the only junior rider competing against adults from Canada and the United States, I became Canadian reserve champion in dressage at the Royal Winter Fair in Toronto.

The General was greatly encouraged by our successes, and agreed to come to Canda once more in the spring of 1963, to continue teaching Bonheur and me. We shared his services in the sand ring at our home with some other interested riders from all over Canada and the United States. I acted as interpreter and felt sorry for both the pupils and the General when he and some of them clashed violently.

"*Im Galopp reiten!*" commanded the General. "Canter!" I translated, for the young American who had received the command. I remembered how, in the summer of 1960, I had been broken in to the teaching of the General. At that time it was Mother who translated the innocent word: "Canter!" Then she and the General started talking and seemed to forget about me. After half an hour of solid cantering around and around the ring, without stirrups, I signalled to Mother that I was tired. She gave the General my message, but he ignored it. After a while, in passing, I indicated that I would fall off if I had to go on any longer. Mother, alarmed, pleaded with the General. "She'll hang on!" the General assured her, and turning his back to me, explained to Mother that he did it all with a purpose. The idea was to make me so tired that I would relax and stop holding on with my legs and ride by balance instead. It had worked. Now, however, the young American cantered twice around the ring, then began to walk. "Did I ask you to stop?" the General challenged. "My horse is tired," the boy answered. The Master gave the pupil a crushing look and ignored him for the rest of the course.

I was gradually becoming aware of the value of the General's approach. The year before, I had been so preoccupied with feeling unhappy that I had let myself be overcome by his personality, concentrating solely on not breaking down. I am glad I managed to remain intact, for the General had much to give, although it was given his way and you were left to accept or reject it. I observed him anew as he worked with the other pupils. He stood six feet tall, his hair sleek and black even at sixty-four. His eagle nose made him stand out anywhere. He was in charge on horseback (and elsewhere) and demanded unconditional obedience.

A military man to the core, the General was always fastidious about certain things, and punctuality was one of them. There was no excuse for being late, he once said, and if a pupil was late he would almost certainly miss his lesson. Tardiness was a sign of disrespect for the teacher. On one occasion one of the guest-pupils dared to be late. The General drew himself up in front of the disconsolate young man, pointed at his watch and proclaimed in German: "I did not come over to Canada to wait for you!"

In the photographs at left, Christilot,
aged two, wears the "frog" costume in which
she made her dance debut in Singapore.
"Since then Mother has called me 'a professional
ham.' "

After her family moved to Canada, Christilot
continued to dance with her mother's troupe.
She appears above in an Oriental number,
dancing on a high school stage during a tour
of northern Ontario.

Christilot, centre, her mother, left, and
another member of their company are seen as
they appeared in "Maria Chapdelaine," a
work choreographed by Mrs. Hanson on a
French-Canadian theme.

Christilot during some quiet
moments with Bonheur.

Bonheur and Christilot are shown
(above left) shortly after Bonheur
was bought in 1959.

In the picture below left, they take
a jump during the first Junior
International Horse Show at Major
Pieregorodzki's Olympic Equestrian
Training Centre at Newmarket.

The photograph above right was
made beside the pond at the Hansons'
home in Oak Ridges.

Christilot's three teachers: Major
Anatole Pieregorodzki (below);
General Hermann von Oppeln
Bronikowski (above left); Egon von
Neindorff (below left).

Christilot and Bonheur execute an extended trot during competition. In order to qualify for the Tokyo Olympics, they had first to receive 55% of a perfect score in an international show. Despite some unforeseen complications they achieved the required marks in an international competition at Rotterdam.

The General bellowed his commands at the top of his lungs at all times, much to the consternation of the neighbours on peaceful Sunday mornings. The General's voice could be heard nine or ten houses further up. At last we were tactfully given to understand that not all the people on our street were interested in taking horseback lessons.

After he had been with us for awhile, the General asked to see a class at Mother's studio. He had stated that he found real pleasure in teaching me because I took directions so well, and I suppose he realized that my dance training with Mother had something to do with this. It was interesting to observe the General's reactions as he watched a class in action. With his scientific approach, he looked at the students not as people with feelings, but as mere vehicles for motion. Pointing at one girl he asked, "Now what do you do to correct those bow-legs?" Mother explained that bow-legs are really the result of a sway-back. By tilting the pelvis and engaging the muscles of the loins, the knees turn slightly out, closing the legs without affecting the straight feet position, and lo and behold! bow-legs become straight legs. From that time forward the General advised everybody, including his own wife, to take lessons from Mother. He himself, however, did not venture to do so.

From May to September the intensive training continued in the sand ring. During these months Bonheur gradually engaged more behind, until he would canter almost without advancing. The extended trot improved; "zig-zag" half passes were practised in trot and canter. Flying changes were done from four-tempo to three- and two-tempo. The pirouettes in canter became smaller. All this was accomplished in a snaffle bridle. Before each competition a week was needed to accustom the thoroughbred to the double bridle, Bonheur's mouth being so small; and to this day he goes better on the snaffle, in contrast to most dressage horses.

In October of 1963 Bonheur and I won the American Horse Shows Association Dressage Medal Class at Washington, D.C. And a month later we became dressage champions of Canada for the first time, at the Royal Winter Fair in Toronto.

Experts say that it takes a very talented horse four years of training to be brought up to the Grand Prix level by a master trainer. However, it takes a rider at least ten years to learn to go through a Grand Prix de Dressage test. I was fourteen when I started working on dressage and would be seventeen by the time of the Tokyo Olympics. Although Bonheur and I were the dressage champions of Canada, I was considered too young to represent the country, seeing that the representatives of the leading countries in dressage—Switzerland, Germany and Russia—were in their forties and fifties. These masters rode young horses of nine and older, while the younger riders between twenty and thirty were mounted on experienced horses who were already being trained before I was born. The combination of the youngest Grand Prix de Dressage rider ever and a very young Grand Prix horse was a little ridiculous to contemplate. However, Canada had to start somewhere in dressage, and it was decided that if I could achieve 55 per cent of the total marks in a top international show, I would qualify for Tokyo.

The day after our victory at the Royal, Bonheur began his usual let-down, in preparation for his winter vacation. The General had begun a little with the passage, but had not touched the piaffe and the flying change every stride. Earlier in our training we had been held up, because Bonheur seemed to go unequally in the hind legs, as if he were lame. The General discovered that my left side was stronger than my right, and that my aids with the left leg caused Bonheur's left hind leg to step forward more, giving the impression he was dragging his right hind leg. "Design an exercise to make her straight!" he commanded Mother. She did, and every evening I had to lie on my stomach on the ground with Mother holding my strong leg. I had to raise my body fifty times, working doubly hard on my weak side. Sure enough, when I was straightened out and exerted an equal pressure on both sides of the horse, Bonheur went straight too! This proves how, especially in advanced dressage, it is imperative that the rider develop all his own muscles equally and systematically.

For the year of 1964, the General accepted a position in Chicago to train Lippizaners. Since I had to be in Europe, the scene of international competition, Mother applied to the Neindorff *Reitinstitut* (Riding Institute) in Karlsruhe, Germany, for a place for Bonheur and me. While waiting for an answer from Herr von Neindorff, I drove up regularly through February and March to Newmarket, where Bonheur was stabled in heated luxury at the Ballard Farms. The first time I went into Mr. Ballard's barn, I thought I was entering a private home and was quite surprised to find horses inside the white, brick building. The huge indoor arena was not far away.

Bonheur always had to be covered with one or two blankets for the cold, windy walk from the barn to the arena. A few steps outside the barn, and he would suddenly interrupt his walk to have a good look at the morning's goings on. First he scrutinized the goats on the far hill. Then, when he had decided they were the same as before, he'd give a nod, and on he would go, close by my side, down to our working quarters. While I fought with the giant sliding doors that led into the arena, Bonny never failed to rub his head vigorously against my back. He wasn't much help in that respect.

Once he had pushed me inside, the game stopped, and he responded to my serious attitude with obedience. First came longeing for twenty to thirty minutes. At a relaxed trot on a large circle, Bonheur would swing around me, tethered by the canvas line in my hand. This was to loosen and stretch his muscles. Responding to my commands, he went from trot to canter and back again, as often as three times in one circle. Once in a while the discipline proved more than he could bear. With a squeal and a jump into the air, all four feet off the ground, he kicked out his repressed exuberance. A corrective word from me brought out a happy snort, then he settled down to resume work. Luckily, neither of us knew just how much still lay ahead of us, or we might have thought twice before agreeing to go on with our destiny.

One happy day arrangements were made to ship us off to Karlsruhe. We still had to learn the most difficult movements called for in the Grand Prix test: the flying change every stride, and the piaffe. We had only seven months before Tokyo.

5   *The* Reitinstitut

The third time our car and trailer passed his stopped truck, the New York milkman realized that our white plates were Canadian and he leaned out into the early morning mist. "Can I help you?" he called. That was a welcome sound to our ears. After driving all night, Daddy and I were not feeling up to disentangling the maze of Kennedy International Airport.

"Where is the ASPCA building?"

"Follow me," the driver said. Perhaps he remembered *his* first time at the huge airport. He shot off into the mist, zooming right and left around sharp bends and stopping for nothing, but seeing that we were no longer right behind him, he finally stopped. His cargo must have turned to buttermilk by that time. At last we drew out of the fog and crept up behind him. More slowly this time, the milk truck led off again, the driver realizing that horses have to be treated more carefully than undelivered milk.

We reached our destination and thanked our guide. A monkey came loping out to greet the new visitor to the Society's quarters, but seeing it was a huge, four-footed beast he screamed and ran back inside. Bonheur was unimpressed by

59

this little demonstration, and more concerned with stretching his legs after the fourteen-hour drive. Ten seconds after being led into his stall, he was rolling in the straw. I smiled. This was normal behaviour for my champion.

After a twelve-hour rest we wrapped bandages carefully around Bonheur's legs, dressed him in a hood with a sheepskin halter and a green blanket that proudly but discreetly proclaimed "Canada," and took him out to the waiting KLM airfreighter. Quietly Bonny followed me up the long ramp specially provided for him. Lowering his head, he stepped down into the belly of the plane, his mordax-studded shoes clinking on the metal floor plates. After manoeuvring around crates and boxes, he was backed into his special stall and quickly fastened in. Then I walked back to the open door of the plane. The ramp had been rolled away. Bonheur whinnied worriedly, but my voice assured him that I wasn't going anywhere.

From the asphalt below Daddy gazed up at me seriously. Smiling through a mist of tears, I returned his wave. In less than twenty-four hours, I would be 3,000 miles away, in Karlsruhe.

Flying is a dangerous business for horses. Too often it ends in tragedy, when a confused and frightened animal becomes violent. Then years of diligent training go for nothing, for the pilot carries a revolver and will use it unhesitatingly if he feels his plane's safety is being endangered.

One by one the motors coughed and spluttered to life. I talked quietly to Bonheur and stroked his neck to keep him calm. Tranquillizing pellets had been given to him two hours before, as the vet had prescribed. I steadied myself on the edge of the stall while the plane taxied out to the runway, lurching occasionally with the uneven pavement. We came to a stop, and each of the four motors in turn was throttled up to full power for the final check. This was the point at which I had been instructed to go to the small seat and fasten myself in. But I stayed next to the stall, reassuring and steadying my precious thoroughbred. It was two years since he had done his last flying. He seemed to say, however, "What's good enough for you is O.K. with me." Finally the motors roared to full power. Gathering speed, we raced towards the yellow lights marking the end of the runway and lifted into the night.

Once more I was setting out on the lonely road of struggle that I hoped would end in achievement. I visualized the figure of my father standing beside his silver-gray car below. He would be gazing at the flashing red light as it banked gently out towards the Atlantic, following it until it disappeared into the night. Then he'd begin the long drive home, the empty trailer behind him.

The noise of the engines reverberated through the cabin. I didn't see the bright lights of Broadway pass beneath us as I coaxed Bonheur back onto his feet, after he had been thrown off balance by the steep climb. Since that take-off he has never again been caught off balance. A seasoned member of the jet-set now, he leans well forward into the gravitational force, nibbling sugar out of my hand, steady and calm throughout.

After our first hour in the air, the customary over-the-Atlantic stillness settled throughout the plane. Eventually the cockpit door opened and the captain came walking aft. After introducing himself he asked, "How is everything?"

"Fine," I said, and looking at Bonheur, added: "His happiness would have been complete if you had ascended more gradually."

"Sorry," the pilot said, "never thought of it. Thanks for the tip."

Bonheur blinked, still under the influence of the tranquillizer, and rubbed his itchy eye against my shoulder. The captain smiled. I guess he saw how close we were. Probably he began to understand why I had been allowed to fly with my horse against the regulations, for persons under twenty-one are not permitted to travel as animal attendants under international airline rules, nor are members of the fair sex. But I had received special permission to accompany my valuable horse.

Night passed quickly. The sun shone through the portholes and the gray ocean seemed very still, 20,000 feet below. Lunch time came and went. I was advised we would land in Amsterdam in two hours. When I opened the bottle of pellets and poured a few into my hand, holding them out to Bonheur, the KLM crew raised their eyebrows in amazement. They were all the more astonished when Bonheur reached down, sniffed and compliantly ate them.

As I faced anew the dangers of going down, when so many horses get hurt, I became conscious of the pitiful weakness of man. I couldn't help praying out loud in the aircraft, quoting the first Bible passage that came to mind: "Be still and know that I am God." And Bonheur *was* still and quiet, unlike two years ago when we had landed in Montreal, and the animal attendant had become covered with blood from fighting him. Finally there was a short squeal from the tires and the airship settled down safely at its home port. The motors roared again, breaking our hurtling momentum.

After two hours on the ground, during which KLM served me an appetizing Dutch meal, Bonheur and I were carried aloft for the short hop over the border to Stuttgart. From there it was a two-hour drive to Karlsruhe. Without my knowledge, however, a zealous plane attendant had removed my important tack trunk in Amsterdam. It would take a week to be located and find its way to Karlsruhe. "We're in Germany," I told Bonheur, thankful for a safe journey. Now I began to worry about my German, which was rusty from lack of use.

A small crowd of horse people awaited our plane's arrival at the Stuttgart airport. It was five in the afternoon, local time. Two men in immaculate riding dress stood at the front of the group, and the shorter of them had a small box under his left arm. The plane eased near to where he stood, then swung around sideways with a short blast from the starboard motors. As I stepped out through the opened door, I decided that one of the two gentlemen must be Mr., or rather "Herr," von Neindorff.

The moment I set foot on the ground, Herr von Neindorff stepped forward, introduced himself, and handed me a box of chocolates. *"Sagen Sie niemand wie alt Sie sind* (Tell nobody how old you are)," were his first words. I was to learn that a rider's age is a factor in the way he is judged in competition. But my first impression at the time was that, somehow, the fact that Bonheur and I were making a bid for the 1964 Olympics was more important in Germany than in my own country. To my amazement, a number of reporters seemed to have been informed about a new horse from Canada, which was trying to catch up with prepared Olympic horses in a ridiculously short time. The question they all asked was: "Do you think you will succeed? Will the horse be ready for the Grand Prix in October?" I told them the truth: "I can't say." When an interviewer asked how old I was, Herr von Neindorff quickly answered for me: "Twenty-one." It was actually

my last day as a sixteen-year-old. Herr von Neindorff introduced me to the gentleman who had accompanied him, a
riding instructor from England who was in Karlsruhe for a
refresher course. As I shook hands, I wondered whether I
came over to him as twenty-one. It was quite a worry, apart
from suddenly having to speak German. Then we were held
up waiting for the government veterinarian who was to check
Bonheur. He arrived very late, and my poor horse caught a
cold before he was allowed to leave the windy airport.

The drive from Stuttgart to Karlsruhe took us over terrible
roads. Herr von Neindorff, the English instructor, the driver
and I were all packed in like sardines in the front of the
truck. I could hear Bonheur occasionally shifting his feet in
the van behind to keep his balance. And I mustn't forget
"Franz Joseph," Herr von Neindorff's mongrel dog, who accompanied him wherever he went, from restaurants to air-
ports. Franz Joseph took up whatever space was left.

It was midnight when the headlamps of the van outlined
the Reitinstitut's stucco-covered buildings. My right leg was
numb from sitting so long in the decrepit old vehicle. It had
no dashboard lights at all and could hardly climb a hill.
Craning my neck from my doubled-up position as we whined
in low gear through the cobblestone courtyard, I tried in
vain to get an idea of the riding school's layout.

Then I got my first surprise. Herr von Neindorff said he
did not have any box stalls! He had only a standing stall for
Bonheur. But I quickly told him that my horse had never
been tied up, that he bit other horses, that he would roll and
hurt himself. The result was that Herr von Neindorff lost no
time switching Bonheur to a loose box.

With the weary traveller done up for the night, I was finally taken to the home where I was to live for the next six

months. I dutifully unpacked my dresses and wardrobe, as Mother had made me promise to do upon arrival. The lady of the house, a grandmother and mother of thirteen, came in to help me and soon took me under her wing. Frau Kuhs, who was seventy-eight, made me feel at home at once. It appeared that there were other Neindorff pupils boarding in her house, since the place was only five minutes' walking distance from the Reitinstitut. My room was very nice, with a comfortable bed, lots of cupboards and a writing desk. The only thing it lacked was a washbasin and mirror. To wash I had to charge along the hallway, hoping that no one else had the same idea at the same time.

For an elderly lady, Frau Kuhs was remarkably alert and agile. She took a genuine interest in her boarders and, without being meddlesome, managed to make them conform to the rules of the house. Later I often admired her concentration and work-power. As I offered her one of Herr von Neindorff's chocolates the first night, she told me that in her opinion "The Maestro" was quite an artist. She could not understand his "caprices," however, such as riding until midnight and giving parties in the stables. My curiosity was aroused, but Frau Kuhs cut me short by pulling the eiderdown blanket over my head and leaving me to rest. Whether because of the six-hour time change, or the excitement of the journey and my new surroundings, sleep would not come. Finally I turned on the light and began to scribble a letter home. "We survived!" I wrote. "Bonheur landed like a real pro. . . ."

When morning came, my problems started. There was no hot water faucet at the sink in the bathroom, which necessitated my washing in ice-cold water. The bath looked very complicated, being one of those gas things which you have to light with a match in order to get hot water. It took a lesson from Frau Kuhs later in the day to teach me how to avoid an explosion. I became a bit homesick for my own bathroom in Canada, where I had any amount of hot water.

After making myself a cup of tea and some toast in Frau Kuhs' kitchen, I was on my way to the stables to see Bonheur. I first checked to see if he had survived the night without getting any cuts or bruises. He looked fine, although a bit tired and tucked up around the belly from the long hours of standing. He had been fed and watered, so I took him for a walk to give him a chance to stretch his legs and have a good look at his new surroundings. Wandering from the back of the building, where Bonheur occupied one of the two portable outside stalls, through the main barn to the front, we found three horses working outside in the sand ring. As we edged closer, an English-speaking voice caught my attention. It was coming from a young teacher who was longeing a girl on horseback. It was a rather pleasant feeling to find someone speaking my language. Later I was introduced to this man, who had a name a mile long, Baron Hobbe van Baerdt van Sminia, a Dutchman who was to become one of my best friends.

Continuing our investigation, we proceeded to the indoor riding hall. The footing inside was a mixture of sand and peat moss, rather deep and soft. The walls were stucco, reaching up into a beautiful domed ceiling, and the large windows on each side and two Dutch doors on one side let in lots of air and light. At the far end stood two pillars, about ten feet high, with leather padding from the top down to about three feet from ground level. On the left wall was a large mirror, to help riders correct their postures and those of their mounts.

"Na, Fräulein Hanson, sind Sie schon da!" The voice of Herr von Neindorff brought me back to the present. I turned

around to find him standing behind me, cigar clenched between his teeth and longeing whip in his hand. He advised
me to keep Bonheur just walking for that first day, but I
could ride if I felt up to it! I certainly did, but then I found
that my boots and saddle and all of Bonheur's gear were
packed in the tack trunk that definitely had *not* landed with
us in Stuttgart. Hasty telephone calls informed us that the
trunk had been unloaded in Amsterdam by mistake, but
steps were taken to get my baggage to the Reitinstitut as soon
as possible.

In borrowed boots, I made my debut on "Aleska," a four-
year-old Hannoveraner, reputed to be the most difficult horse
in the barn. Did I have any experience with young horses?
Herr von Neindorff wanted to know. Yes, I had a four-year-
old colt of my own in Canada.

Aleska, a ticklish mare, was indeed a problem. If your
hands were too hard, she immediately got behind the bit. If
your hands were too soft, she fell apart at once. She was also
quite temperamental and stopped and reared, if not handled
with care. Probably Herr von Neindorff had chosen her because he wanted to see how I would manage. Aleska behaved,
and Herr von Neindorff seemed pleased.

Next I was sent to sit in the office, in German called *das
Büro*, a heated space behind glass windows overlooking the
arena. From the Büro, Herr von Neindorff, who was nick-
named *der Chef* by the students, taught his classes. His voice
resounded through the arena, which was often filled with
appropriate riding music. For the time being, however, he
entered the arena on foot alone, while a groom brought in
"Mars," a huge Trakehner. I looked forward eagerly to seeing my new teacher ride! What I saw exceeded my wildest
dreams. I silently recognized in Herr von Neindorff a true

artist. Watching the "giant battle-machine" (the name I had given Mars at first sight) doing four pirouettes in sequence at a canter, I counted six perfect steps each time the horse went through 360 degrees. It was almost too much when he was halted, in order to allow the students to examine the perfect circle made by the pivoting hind hooves.

"Does Bonheur pirouette as well?" Herr von Neindorff asked me.

"Ah . . . he's been on vacation," I mumbled. The Master's face betrayed nothing as he nodded in understanding agreement. Continuing to move around the mirror-decked wall of the arena, Mars went into an elevated passage, while Herr von Neindorff sat erect in the saddle. Turning into the centre the horse began piaffing, not only in place, but in pirouettes too!

"In the '64 test we just need to do ten piaffe steps," I thought as I admired this endless execution of the piaffe, one of the most difficult Grand Prix movements. The big Trakehner snorted, his 'trot-on-the-spot' reminiscent of ancient battle scenes in which a knight's mount tramples a fallen enemy rider to death.

"One thing anyway," I thought to myself, "North American thoroughbreds top anything over here for looks." Just then Herr von Neindorff dismounted and motioned me to join him in the arena. A most gorgeous Italian thoroughbred was brought in, the mare "Dourina." I suspect I was longed on her because she was not easy to sit. The longeing was done in a strong, almost extended trot in a very small circle, without reins or stirrups, of course. What a session! The skin on the inside of my knees was rubbed off from that one experience, which marked the beginning of my continued use of band aids all through the Karlsruhe training period. But I ended my first day happy in the knowledge that I was studying in the best school in Europe.

It was Herr von Neindorff's difficult task to bring Bonheur up to Grand Prix level from the point at which the General had left off. The General had begun teaching Bonheur the passage first, rather than the piaffe. According to some experts, the General was proceeding in the wrong order. They say that you can push a horse from the piaffe into the passage, but not vice versa. This is still a hotly contested question, with one group of trainers claiming that the piaffe should definitely be taught first, because the horse's carrying muscles must be developed before he is asked to carry *and* push simultaneously, as required in the passage. The other school maintains that it is a completely individual matter, since some horses show more inclination towards the passage than the piaffe.

My own observation is still that all horses that can do the piaffe can more or less execute a passage, but the reverse is not always so. At any rate, argument continues as to whether the passage is indeed the more difficult movement. I feel that the conformation of a horse is a deciding factor in the question. For example, the heavier cross-bred horse with strong quarters can learn the piaffe more easily, while the thoroughbred type sometimes has difficulty in lowering his quarters and carrying his weight. On the other hand, because he is a lighter horse the thoroughbred finds it easier to carry himself with elevation in the passage. But all the same, not every horse can be taught both of these most difficult movements of the *Haute École*.

In the light of the foregoing, it is understandable that the General had taken on a bet with a friend that Bonheur would never learn the piaffe. He was also dubious about the possibility of his mastering the flying change every stride. All I can say is that the General rightly foresaw trouble, but I am grateful that my horse and I persevered, for thanks to the untiring efforts of Herr von Neindorff, Bonheur succeeded in learning all the required movements of the Grand Prix de Dressage. When we arrived in Tokyo six months later, only the piaffe needed drastic improvement, since Bonheur had to be extremely excited to do it correctly. I remember once coming back from the practice ring in the Olympic Equestrian Park. All of a sudden a child jumped out of the bushes as we were passing. Bonheur, startled, began to piaffe beautifully, and it took some time before I could persuade him to stop. He seemed utterly pleased with himself, but he had to pay for it with terrible muscle pain the next day.

The piaffe can be compared with the popular Russian dance step in which the dancer, with arms folded, kicks out his legs alternately from a squatting position. It takes lots of muscle strength to execute the step, as well as the exuberance to perform it with expression. Excitement sends any horse into piaffing in the initial stages of learning this high school movement. It is an avenue for the release of excess energy. However, if it becomes a habit for a horse to piaffe at the least provocation, it reveals faulty instruction. The reaction resembles that of a punchdrunk boxer.

The name "Bonheur" means "good luck" as well as "happiness." Indeed, how lucky we were to have crossed paths with Herr von Neindorff, a master of the piaffe. He once asserted laughingly: "I can teach a donkey piaffe!" And watching der Chef do this high school movement with different breeds was most interesting.

To give me a deep seat I was longed five or six times a day. Sometimes these sessions represented sheer hell, but that was

Filatov, the Russian gold-medal winner at the 1960 Olympics,
gives Christilot some pointers at Tokyo.

A Free Dancer's Approach to Dressage

Alternately tilting (lower photo) and relaxing (upper photo) the pelvis
helps the rider discover which muscles participate in the bracing of the back.
Note in the lower photo how the central contraction of the spine extends
the muscle action to the neck muscles, shortening the back of the neck and
raising the chin, and to the leg muscles, bending the knees.

Learning to "post" on the ground to music strengthens the leg and
back muscles for the "chair" seat and develops the rider's feeling
for rhythm. The photo *above* demonstrates the right and the
wrong (girl at left) ways to do this exercise. *Below* the incorrect
position (girl at left) with the seat stuck out and the leg muscles passive
is contrasted with the correct seat (right) in which the back is kept
completely straight and the leg muscles are active.

The connected and the disconnected walk contrasted:
Above—Connected: The knee of the active leg is bent, the heel lifted,
the back of the neck shortened, and the chin raised by the central contraction
of the spine. As the leg moves forward the weight travels vertically above it.
The foot touching the ground toe first rolls from toe to heel and the leg
and neck are again passively stretched.
Below—Disconnected: The moving leg is dragged forward from the hip,
the foot landing heel first. The weight which has remained over the
inactive leg is then transferred to the moving leg, now the inactive leg.

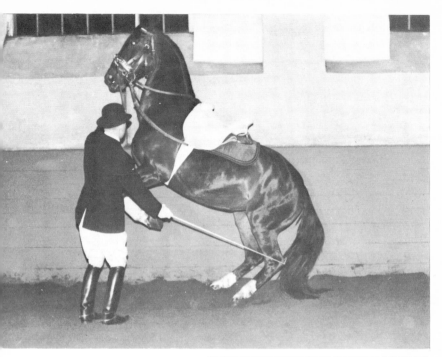

Herr von Neindorff at the *Reitinstitut* in Karlsruhe training "Luna" to execute a levade, one of the "above-the-ground" movements, which are not required in the Olympic test.

This view of Bonheur executing a half-pass to the right at the trot shows how the diagonal pairs of legs cross during this movement. Note how the horse is flexed around the rider's inside (right) leg.

Bonheur on a snaffle executing a natural extended trot (above) exhibits the clear-cut rhythm of the diagonals working in precise unison. Note the rider in training position without stirrups maintains a straight line between her elbow and the horse's mouth. Compare the length of stride in the extended trot with the shortened stride of the passage (below) in which the powerful thrust of the diagonals in unison maintains the basic tempo of the trot. Note tension causing the horse to resist the bit.

how Herr von Neindorff's best riders acquired their fantastic seats: ride, ride, ride, and ride some more, until out of sheer desperation you find the lowest point and sit tight, or else get bounced to death. It seemed an eternity before I got the feeling of the correct seat, but what a difference it made to my security in the saddle. I knew that when I returned to Canada, my riding would be unrecognizable. I made up my mind to make the most of this European training, because I felt there was an obligation to fulfil to my country. There was so much I would be able to introduce. My horizons had opened out. I wanted the public to see horses going on long reins, horses piaffing, doing levades and flying changes.

On top of my private lessons with Herr von Neindorff I was allowed to join all other classes during the day. One of the most enjoyable rides at the Institute was the *Abteilung*, or "Group Ride," to music. The very first time I took part in it I was mounted on "Landgraf," a large, seventeen-hand Holsteiner. Behind the glass windows of the Büro, a group of students had gathered around der Chef, who was giving commands through the amplifier. Restraining my horse and trying to keep the correct distance behind the horse in front, I couldn't help noticing how some of the riders were leaning over the ledge. They were intent on the last of the fifteen pupils now doing sitting trot through the diagonal. I felt their critical gaze. I knew full well that, since I was a newcomer and a possible Olympic candidate, the top riders would want to size me up. I had been told nothing about my mount. "Undoubtedly," I figured, "this horse must have a quirk somewhere."

Commands rolled out through the loudspeakers. In those first days I had no clue as to what Herr von Neindorff was saying. The combination of local dialect and electronic distortion was too much for my unaccustomed ear. Furtively looking around, I attempted to follow those in front. *"Fräulein Hanson!"* was often heard in the arena that morning, as Herr von Neindorff took special care to break me in to the routine quickly. So we rode, spaced evenly one behind the other, men and women going through, down, around, and across the arena in varying figures and gaits. The last fifteen minutes of the hour-long lesson were spent on the canter. In turn each rider moved off, swinging down the diagonal and performing a flying change at the letter X, the centre.

"Fräulein Hanson, c-a-n-t-e-r please." The watchers in the Büro stirred and became more intent. Bonheur had been trained to canter off the inside leg, rather than the usual outside leg. It was embarrassing for me to break off twice on the wrong lead on a differently trained horse. The third time I reverted to the old Pony Club trick. I pushed the quarters in, and the horse couldn't help but strike off on the right lead. Finally in gear, I swung around the edge and turned down the diagonal.

The rider's timing has to be exact, especially for the one-tempo flying changes. Being off a hundredth of a second, just once, multiplies rapidly in geometric progression to the point where the horse's rhythm is destroyed, so that after the third or fourth change the horse stumbles, or only changes in front. As I travelled on the big steed towards X, I looked unperturbed. Just as I wanted to apply the aid—click, the horse changed beautifully. I had not done anything, but it seemed that cunning old Landgraf knew Herr von Neindorff's mind and obliged in advance with perfect timing! Again I went through the diagonal, doing a second lovely change. The faces in the Büro showed disappointment, mixed with grudging admiration.

Later Hobbe, the Dutchman, told me that what they were really waiting for was the tremendous unexpected buck that Landgraf never failed to give after a rider had influenced him to change. I had spoiled their expectations of seeing me lunged four feet into the air. Once, however, I managed to give Landgraf the aid before he could change of his own accord. Boom! Surprised, I stayed with the horse as he seemed to fly upward and then came down on the other lead. Relieved smiles broke out. The consensus of opinion among the riders in the Büro: "Weak seat, but she certainly has a sensitive feel for horses."

As soon as Bonheur was settled, Herr von Neindorff started on the piaffe. There was much outside interest in our progress at the Institute, not only from reporters and photographers, but also from curious German equestrians. One of my colleagues at the Institute received a letter from a well-known German dressage judge, asking him to report on Bonheur and disclose his weaknesses. I thought it rather strange. It reminded me of an instance in the summer of 1963, when the General was training Bonheur in Canada. Visitors from the States took a film of Bonheur working, which greatly upset the General. "They have come to spy on him," he said, grumbling about all the intrigues that always seemed to go on during Olympic preparations. We thought the General was still confused about his past war experiences.

However, as time went by I began slowly to understand what it was all about. With the cavalry disappearing in Europe, dressage is in decline. At present there are about forty horses and riders in the whole world able to go through a Grand Prix de Dressage test. Only a handful of trainers are left who can teach a talented horse piaffe and passage. I would say also that only a handful of experts are left who can evaluate dressage properly. (We were lucky to have one on the North American continent in the late Mr. Richard Watjen.) Some judges have only a theoretical knowledge of their subject, not supported by practical experience.

The most highly rated competitors in the Grand Prix are usually in their thirties, forties or fifties. At Tokyo most of these masters rode young horses, whereas all the younger riders used experienced, older horses who began their training before Bonheur and I were born. The idea of a seventeen-year-old attempting to make her debut in the Grand Prix de Dressage on an inexperienced, nine-year-old horse seemed ludicrous to many. Thus Major Pieregorodzki had advised Mother, when I was fifteen, to start saying I was a few years older. Herr von Neindorff also thought it bad politics to expose my youth and so create a prejudice against me because of my inexperience. This prejudice was and was not justified, for through my education in natural movement I had acquired the muscle control and the understanding of the laws of movement that come to most riders only after long years in the saddle.

To learn the piaffe, Bonheur was worked in long reins, in the hand from the ground, and from the saddle, at first not longer than ten minutes at a time. Herr von Neindorff found out quickly how far he could go before the horse would fight, and stopped shortly before that point was reached.

The piaffe is really an independent gait. The term "trot-on-the-spot" is actually misleading. The piaffe movement does not resemble a trot, nor is "on-the-spot" to be taken literally. The dressage piaffe, unlike the circus piaffe movement, should be executed moving forward a half-hooflength with each step. Coming from the lumbar region—the centre of movement in the horse's body—it is extremely difficult to

achieve. Tremendous strength is required in the hindquarters of the horse to execute it correctly. When the movement
is done correctly the horse is highly collected, with the
haunches well under. This makes for a light forehand, allow-
ing the legs to move alternately and rhythmically upward,
while advancing a half-hooflength.

Circus-trained horses execute the piaffe in a disconnected
way. Using the whip wrongly, the circus trainer touches the
horse's front legs in order to get the elevation. The result is
artificial. The horse remains uncollected and although the
front legs are lifted higher, the rest of the anatomy is not
engaged. The haunches do not remain level, but swing from
side to side. Anatomically speaking, the correctly executed
piaffe has its starting point from the back, while the wrongly
executed piaffe originates from the horse's knees, in the fashion of a high-stepping majorette.

At regular intervals reporters kept coming to the Institute
to interview me and take pictures of Bonheur. A man from
the local radio station came to tape an interview with Herr
von Neindorff and me. I never imagined I would be speaking
German on the radio. It went on the air as a sports extra the
following night.

As a teacher Herr von Neindorff was much quieter and
more friendly than the General. His marvellous sense of
humour, passionate love of horses, and his admirable coolness
acted as a tonic on me. This is not to say that the final stretch
to the Grand Prix was a path of roses. In my memory the
Reitinstitut will always be a place of tormented happiness.

I was now riding six or seven hours a day. Five more horses
were assigned to me to give me more experience. Sometimes I
was too tired to eat and fell into bed without dinner. Hobbe
did not approve of that and he functioned as a self-appointed

guardian angel. He stimulated my appetite by taking me to wonderful restaurants, where he introduced me to champagne mixed with orange juice and "shashlik" (different sorts of meat on a stick), eaten to the accompaniment of whining Gypsy violins.

Hobbe had studied sociology in Geneva and Paris and had travelled all over the world. Speaking four languages fluently, he was Elegance in person to me. He continually amused me with his dry remarks, which were a cross between English and German humour. I got to know all the stable gossip from him. I enjoyed having someone to talk to while eating. In the international scene he knew everyone from the Hindu dancer Ram Gopal and Spanish dancer Jose Greco to Johnny Mathis and Pat Smythe. He had taken part in the Badminton Three-Day Event and had been on the Dutch team. He was also one of the select group of boys chosen to go dancing and sailing with Princess Irene of Holland before her marriage to a Spanish prince. As a true Dutchman, he was greatly shocked by the marriage. Very much the aristocrat, he would not get his hands dirty and had fits when Bonheur rubbed his head on his riding jacket. He was good at the rhumba and mambo. Pleasantly surprised to find I could follow his wildest steps, he promised in a weak moment to exercise with me, but could never bring himself to lie on the ground.

My moods still went from joy to depression and back again in a minute. One moment I would thank God for my good fortune, as I tried to absorb as much as possible of Herr von Neindorff's training. The great riding hall, Strauss waltzes soothing horse and rider, Bonheur going between long reins, a trainer walking behind him, and der Chef with two whips alongside. . . . I felt as though I were moving in a dream. But sometimes the dream became a nightmare. I had some horrible scenes with Bonheur on his piaffe work. Once I found myself against the wall, with Herr von Neindorff standing beside me with a whip. Bonheur had decided he had had enough and lunged away. The whip cracked and dust flew as Herr von Neindorff roared: "Back to the wall! Back! Back!" So I, without stirrups, tried to get us back to the wall. The whip snarled around my waist, and Herr Von Neindorff screamed, "Sit!" while Bonheur got a wallop from behind. This made him piaffe beautifully for some moments, but all of a sudden I seemed to be galloping backwards as the horse tried again to get away from the wall. Then the screaming started all over again and the whip curled around Bonheur's ankles as we flew forward once more....

As I nursed my aching body in bed at night, I wondered whether, when Bonheur and I performed the piaffe in the future, people would ever guess how we had fought, sweated, and cried to get it out of him. A question repeated itself in my head: Why oh why do I go through with it all? And the answer came from the past: It took you a long time to master the flying change, remember? Take defeat until victory comes. And come it will, if you don't run. The voice of the General came back to me: *"Immer weiter! Immer weiter!* (Always further! Always further!) "* It wasn't the riding, it was what it stood for: overcoming difficulties! It was the overcoming of fear, the perseverance and endurance, the hope and faith, qualities that have to be developed if they are to become part of the individual character.

At the time my arms felt like lead. And my seat bones! I wished they did not belong to me. But I realized that poor Bonheur must have muscle pain too. For some time after the piaffe work had started he had just kept rearing. Herr von

Neindorff said it proved that the weak spot had been reached. "First thing in the morning I'll rub his legs and back with alcohol," I thought.

The next day the attendants at the Institute teased me. They said they wished they were Bonheur. "He gets better care than the average husband!" they exclaimed.

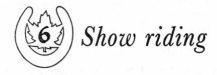 *Show riding*

At the Reitinstitut the annual *Veranstaltung* or "Open House Exhibition" was the high point of the year. A performance of the highest classical calibre and dedicated to the preservation of dressage in its purity, it was scheduled to run for three days. It came to a climax on the Saturday, when many prominent persons were in attendance. Because it was carried on without competition and because the horses used in the performance were almost all trained by Herr von Neindorff, the level of riding was extremely high.

Nowadays many horses exhibit untrue, cramped, circus-like movements because their owners show them too soon, without bothering to lay a solid foundation in training. Amidst the intrigues and the high-pressured competition, it is a welcome relief to see riders performing just because they enjoy it. The Reitinstitut's Veranstaltung has acquired a very good name for itself through the years. Many months in advance, Herr von Neindorff started training for the event that would bring together the elite of the European riding world. Since I had never witnessed anything of this nature before, the show became one of the highlights of my life.

That I had set my sights on Tokyo did not interfere at all

with Herr von Neindorff's programme. There was always a number for a Grand Prix horse in his show. As it turned out, Bonheur and I performed a *Pas de Trois* with two other Grand Prix riders.

In preparation for the event, der Chef had me riding as many different horses per day as possible. The differences in handling each horse widened my experience and gave me a better seat. For instance, there was "Belisar," a huge ox that even big men had difficulty in holding together. But he surprised everyone with the way he could go when well ridden. I had to practise collection and flying changes on him. The point behind it was that if I could collect such a heavy animal and come through on him with flying changes, I would be able to do it twice as well on the light Bonheur.

Then there was the Lippizaner "Kaiser Franz." I learned to adore him, although my first impression was that he reminded me of an undersized milk-wagon horse. He had surprisingly soft gaits, round and roly-poly. But what a neck he had! So massive! The lesson I had to learn on him was to keep his head down. He was easy to sit, however, far easier than Bonheur. Kaiser Franz was also Hobbe's favourite mount. Hobbe affectionately called him "Kaiserle" (Little Emperor). Kaiserle had only one fault: he could reach his eyes with his tongue!

For six months I submitted myself to the strongest discipline of my life. In the end I reached a point where I just walked, ate and rode in a daze. I stopped worrying about aches and pains, concentrating with the last energy I had on just keeping going. I was up at 6:30 every morning to be at the stables at 7:15. Half an hour was needed to clean Bonheur and put his tack and bandages on. Then began my private lesson with Herr von Neindorff. These morning work-outs consisted usually of suppling and collecting exercises, as well as special exercises on pirouettes, two-tracks and flying changes. By 9:30 Bonheur had been cooled out and cleaned and left to enjoy his second breakfast of the day. I, however, was mounted on the longe on either "Isulana," a Lippizaner mare, or "The Swede." How these longeing sessions hurt the insides of my legs! It was awful, but Herr von Neindorff remarked brightly that it was a sign that I had the right muscles in action.

Eleven o'clock found Herr von Neindorff on his grey Andalusian stallion; Ouve, the school instructor, on "Zucha;" and me on the third stallion, "Jarvado." This was one ride that always gave me a lift as we trotted, cantered and circled to music.

At half past one we were allowed an hour break for lunch, then I had to have Bonheur ready for his piaffe work-out. I often tried to put myself in Bonheur's place, having to do the almost impossible job of learning in a matter of months what other horses learn in years. Not accustomed to being worked from the ground, because the General did not believe in handwork, Bonheur was very suspicious at first of the new approach. Herr von Neindorff often expressed his regret that he had not met us both earlier, in which case much that now seemed strange to Bonheur would have been routine for him. As it was, the pillars appalled him. The pillars are a device for teaching the piaffe introduced in France in the seventeenth century by Pluvinel, who is considered the first great riding master after Xenophon. Pluvinel was reputed to be an accomplished horseman at the age of seventeen. He is especially known for the recorded dialogue between Louis XIII and himself, entitled *L'Instruction du Roi* (1623). In it the use and abuse of Pluvinel's invention is discussed. The horse is taught to trot on the spot while tied up between two strong pillars, with special reins looped through rings on a well padded noseband and headstall.

Herr von Neindorff began with holding Bonheur between one pillar and himself. Utterly calm, equipped with his whip and cigar, he gave commands to a groom and Wolfgang Keil, an advanced rider who owned a horse boarded at the Reitinstitut. Bonheur had his longeing girth and side reins on. I stood with a box of sugar in my hand. Every time Bonheur obliged, I was to run forward and give him a reward. The word "Brav!" was my cue to spring into action.

"*Also Los!* (Begin!)" shouted Herr von Neindorff.

After Bonheur had done a couple of steps between Herr von Neindorff and the post, the groom was told to attach the other longe so that the horse was actually between two human pillars. The whip sizzled, Bonheur lunged forward, the ropes pulled tight, a few hurried steps in piaffe. . . . "Brav!" His ears flipped back and he stood motionless. "*Zucker!* (Sugar!)" and I came running forward. At first Bonheur, who had never been given sugar rewards on the theory that candy-feeding teaches a horse to nip, spewed out the sweets in disgust. Afterward he accepted the stuff, but he may have done this just to please us. Animals are funny that way. We once had a dying chihuahua that ate out of our hand because she saw it made us happy to think she was getting better. Bonheur does not enjoy sugar very much. He prefers carrots. More than the sugar, I think, he enjoyed being given a chance to rub his knee with his nose. However this may be, the procedure was repeated over and over again until the horse was dripping and Herr von Neindorff's shirt stuck to his back.

On these occasions Bonheur was sometimes worked on

long reins with Wolfgang behind and Herr von Neindorff alongside with the whip. Bonheur did the passage along the wall, but he pulled away at times. *"Nicht doch!* (Not that way!) " Herr von Neindorff screamed at Bonheur. Wolfgang then managed to get the horse back to where he was and continue the work. As soon as Bonheur had performed some beautiful round steps, he was stripped of his tack right there in the arena and allowed to roll. "Wash him and walk him out," Herr von Neindorff commanded, believing always in sending a horse back to his stall in a happy frame of mind. Then he himself left the arena like a matador, wringing wet, whip in hand and cigar clenched between his teeth. Five minutes later he was back riding another horse.

I too had to ride more horses, either training alone or in group instruction. Between six and seven I went home or to a restaurant for dinner and often came back to ride again until nine or ten. I became accustomed to having back aches, leg aches and many other aches continually. I was awake but not quite clear in the head. "I am pushing you to your limits," Herr von Neindorff said. "The more you can take, the better for you."

As if things were not complicated enough, the Canadian Olympic Equestrian Committee insisted upon my competing in international shows. Before sending me to Tokyo, they had to have tangible proof that Bonheur and I would indeed be up to the high standard required for the Grand Prix. Never having ridden the Grand Prix test in competition, never even having been in a senior, international event (I was too young), I was a very "dark" horse. Understandably, the Committee wondered if I would crack under the strain. No one of my age had dreamt of attempting the Grand Prix. Finally the Committee decided to let me go to Tokyo if I achieved 55 per cent of the total points required in an international test.

Herr von Neindorff, however, was of the opinion that time taken off to show would upset my already crammed training schedule. Time became a barrier between the Committee and the frantically working trio of Herr von Neindorff, Bonheur and me. Letters, cables and phone calls flew and crackled back and forth across the Atlantic. The piaffe progressed painfully, for although we did our very best, muscles can develop only so much at a time.

I refused to give in to discouragement. I felt so stupid sometimes, so crude and ridiculous. For days, sometimes for weeks, nothing went right. Then suddenly it would work! There were moments of perfection, of sheer exhilaration. Herr von Neindorff stepped up the programme, now scolding, now praising me. There was something very satisfying when I got off Bonheur, absolutely exhausted, and Herr von Neindorff said, "Was gut! It's coming!" My heart leapt and I was ready to try it again and again.

I also began my work on long reins. I never realized how fast a horse went until I tried to walk behind one! It was really an experience. Afterwards my legs were just numb.

The hardest daily sessions, however, were those with Bonheur. In the piaffe-passage-piaffe work-outs, I got cramps in my legs and sometimes I could not stretch my arms. The muscles knotted. I repeatedly came close to falling off and thought every time that I could see the ground coming. But we stuck it out. When we finished, both completely soaked, I did everything I could to help Bonheur keep his nerves: walking in the country, letting him eat grass, hosing his legs with cold water, rubbing him with absorbine, bandaging him.

It is said that you learn the strength of your character in

time of crisis. It was typical of Bonheur not to break down. Herr von Neindorff was often worried about him, because he felt that for a young horse he had gone through quite a lot, including the race track experience that alone drives many horses crazy. But although Bonheur had developed that "look" in his eyes that every Grand Prix horse has, he retained his *joie de vivre*.

One morning, after I had worked quite late the night before and been told I could sleep in, I arrived at the barn at 9 a.m. Bonheur looked wide awake and rather perky. The horse attendant told me that he had gone out earlier all by himself. What had happened was this. Ouve had been grooming him outside his stall when suddenly something fell off the roof. Bonheur broke his halter with a lunge backwards and gaily cantered away over the stone floor through the main barn to the back paddock, waking up all the other horses. The paddock was fenced in, so that he could not go anywhere. He still had his night bandages on. They tried and they coaxed, they bribed and they threatened, but no one could come near Mr. Canada! He ate grass quietly until someone was almost in reach of him, then simply turned his hindquarters to the intruder and ran off to another spot. In his own time he returned without further ado to his box stall and there the drama ended. He worked especially well that morning.

Mother, who had taken two weeks' leave from her school in Toronto to visit me, was delighted to see Bonheur so fit and happy. She arrived on a Sunday, the day that the Reitinstitut was deserted and nobody was riding except Herr von Neindorff and me. Late in the afternoon she was sitting in the Büro, looking down into the empty arena. The music of Mozart's country dances came over the loudspeaker.

Eventually the gates opened. A groom led in the Andalusian stallion, Zucha. Prancing and dancing, Zucha did a natural passage, arching his beautiful neck and holding out his long, full tail. Then the gates opened again and I appeared, leading in Jarvado. While I closed the gate he moved in a natural piaffe. Just then the groom led Zucha past the mirror. When the stallion saw his own reflection, he acted as though a rival was facing him. Suddenly rearing, he caught the groom off guard and jumped loose. The next thing I remember is seeing the onrushing Zucha with a feverish look in his eye, mane and tail flying. The second vision was that of Jarvado leaping wildly in the air. I must be endowed with a marvellous sense of self-preservation, for without hesitation I jumped the five-foot gate leading out of the arena.

Mother had looked on aghast at seeing her only daughter being rushed by a stallion. Now the groom stood immobile, as he had been trained to do in such situations. The two "boys" let go and tore around the place, shrieking the way only stallions do, now and then darting straight towards the human statue. Soon both animals reared up on their hind legs, pawing in the air, preparing for an honest-to-goodness fight.

At that moment Herr von Neindorff entered with firm but calm strides from the end of the hall. Speaking softly in a combination of baby- and lover's talk, he gradually quieted the two horses down, calling them *"Liebchen."* Getting hold of Zucha, der Chef gave the groom a chance to catch Jarvado. Herr von Niendorff then picked up a lock of tail hair that had been ripped out in the heat of the battle and gave it as a memento to Mother. Next he motioned me, still standing on the other side of the gate, to mount.

Mother was appalled that Herr von Neindorff let me

mount the wild "beast" and for a moment got panicky when the groom left the arena. But then she became conscious once more of the exquisite music of Mozart that had never stopped playing. When she saw that both teacher and pupil had regained control of the situation, she thought an ancient, classical picture had come to life before her eyes. Delighted by a scene, as she later put it, of "superb courage, elegance, beauty and strength," she couldn't help noticing the great improvement in my riding.

Mother remarked that something of Herr von Neindorff had rubbed off on me. I was riding "with my back" and had taken to cooing to my mount, making horsey noises, "prrr . . . rrrt," to calm him as I followed my teacher, trotting and cantering to the time of the music. I could now sit to bucking without difficulty, until the stallion settled down to work and arched his neck beautifully, as if he had wanted to oblige in the first place.

Mother, always tortured by unco-ordinated riding, could relax for once and give herself over to her reveries. Although this was the first time that she had watched her teenage daughter ride in a Karlsruhe riding hall, she had the strange feeling that she recognized the scene in front of her. Perhaps it was a vision from one of her dreams. Suddenly Herr von Neindorff's voice brought her back to the world. He wanted to know if we could join him for dinner. We could. And so, after the ride at 9, we made our way to the Eden Hotel, squeezing ourselves and Franz Joseph into the Volkswagen.

When artists meet, they speak a language of the spirit. Herr von Neindorff and Mother, although of different temperaments, understood each other perfectly and compared notes. Both were devoted to their art. They drank to the truth and to the piaffe.

It was a pity Mother had to leave before the Veranstaltung. Herr von Neindorff worked frantically to co-ordinate his riders and horses. The barns even received a face-lifting, to match the complete whitewashing of the interiors. Everything was in a turmoil, numbers only half-made, horses going lame, riders wanting this horse or refusing to ride that horse. Poor Herr von Neindorff was tearing his hair and looking very tired. The programme he had designed was just as hard on him as stage shows were on Mother.

It was Mayday, a national holiday in Germany. Nobody worked, no mail was being delivered and people were coming home at 8 o'clock, drunk, sleepy and in taxis. Der Chef, however, brought out the special equipment used only for exhibitions, which, holiday or not, had to be cleaned.

Relieved that the Master's attention was momentarily off me and Bonheur, I took time to drink a Coke and make myself comfortable among the saddles and bridles surrounding me. Just then Wolfgang Keil came sauntering by. "You are a lazy one!" he exclaimed. "Every time I see you, you are eating or drinking."

Whereupon I retorted, "And every time I see you, you ought to be in school, but you aren't."

Without answering, Wolfgang picked up his tack and dropped it in a heap in front of me. "Here," he said bigheartedly, "you may clean this too!" The next moment he jumped away from the kick which flew in his direction.

"My, you Canadians are a wild bunch!" he said amiably. He sat down. "Is it true that you hope to make the 1964 Olympics?"

I smiled. "I suppose you think it is sheer gall for me to even think of Tokyo with my experience . . . and a horse as young as Bonheur."

"You said it," he admitted, more frank than polite. Squinting through his glasses, and looking like a scholar, he said: "Do you realize that most of the riders here have all at one time or another cherished the same ideals, without ever seeing their dreams come true? It is not only a question of handling horses, difficult as that may be. It is the handling of human relationships which is much harder. I am speaking of 'politics.' Even when you and Bonheur do get ready to ride the Grand Prix, you have no hope of conquering all the other factors."

He looked serious and so did I. I told him I knew what he meant, that I was acquainted with discrimination like anyone else. But I was glad I had not allowed myself to be intimidated by it, for if I had I would not have been there that day. I understood that the only person to compete with was myself. I remembered when, at the age of eleven, I had failed to receive a ribbon I felt I had deserved. A complete stranger approached me, and witnessing my fight to keep back the tears, said sympathetically, "Don't cry. I saw your ride. And you will go a long, long way."

I realized then that only I could be the accurate judge of my achievements. The confidence one has or does not have can never be given or taken away by the criticism of others. I told Wolfgang about Major Pieregorodzki. The Major had always distinguished between people who *rode* horses and those who only *talked* horses. All the intrigues in the world could not stop the riding ones, he had told me.

The Veranstaltung was to start with a parade and a salute to the public. Herr von Neindorff had chosen to ride Bonheur to open the evening. To the solemn strains of the music of Handel, Bonheur came in, with six black quadrille horses behind him. They lined up, Herr von Neindorff saluted and the director of the Association for the Advancement of the Art of Riding (*Die Gesellschaft zur Forderung der Reitkunst*), made a speech. Bonheur came in as if he had always been leading armies. While Herr von Neindorff stood at attention, he remained as calm and unruffled as ever. It was really a beautiful sight.

Following this, horses were walked on the line to draw the public's attention to the various breeds and the differences in conformation and gaits. For this part of the show Herr von Neindorff had chosen Bonheur as an example of an American thoroughbred. He also showed an Italian and a German thoroughbred, the East Prussian horses from Sweden and Germany, some Hannoveraners, Holsteiners, and Lippizaners, and my favourite Andalusian stallions from Portugal.

Then the systematic training of a dressage horse was exhibited, starting with three young horses being longed in different corners. After that a group of young horses was shown from the saddle, one behind the other in a long line, in the fundamental walk, trot and canter. This group was a bit unpredictable, for, being young, they were almost always in high spirits. Sometimes even the simple gaits could prove too much for some "baby," and he would squeal his delight and add a buck for good measure, drawing laughter from the audience as his reward.

Next came one of the most difficult numbers. Three horses performed long rein work, i.e. they executed movements such as collected walk, trot and canter, and all the two-track movements, while being directed by their trainers from behind. The trainers walked behind them with two long reins, running from the horse's head to just behind his rump. After that came the Pas de Trois, three horses at Grand Prix level executing under their riders all two-track movements, flying changes, pirouettes, collected and extended gaits. This was the number Bonheur and I were in.

Bonheur had improved tremendously. His canter, which the General used to call *"herrlich* (glorious),"* had become even rounder and more precise, so that I heard the public murmur *"wunderschön"* as we cantered around. But while I tried my best not to have Bonheur look too far behind the other two horses, the reviews in the paper the next morning made me gasp. Under the caption: "Canadian Master Introduced," the article said: "Specially starred was the Canadian rider Christilot Hanson, in a Pas de Trois with her nine-year-old thoroughbred Bonheur. The trio executed half-pass in canter, pirouettes and flying changes in perfection. The two other riders of the Institute did not remain far behind the beautiful accomplishments of the young Canadian. Their dressage figures were at least equally good in impulsion." I shuddered! My work was far from "perfection."

At the conclusion of our act, all horses that could do the piaffe, passage or levade were brought in to demonstrate their skills. This was indeed a beautiful sight, the spotlights following the different horses as they piaffed or picking out the beautiful mare standing in a perfect levade, holding the position with the whole weight on the hindquarters, and the front legs in the air for what seemed an interminable length of time. As she came down, a discerning eye could catch Herr von Neindorff quickly rewarding her efforts with a lump of sugar.

The climax of an unforgettable evening was now at hand. The lights dimmed and the quadrille entered to a classical march. The six black horses, all equipped with white brow bands on their gleaming double bridles and white bandages neatly wrapped around the front legs, captivated me by their grace. This was precision riding of the highest calibre. I had never dreamed that such a thing was possible.

What thrilling new experiences lay before the Canadian public! If only I could bring them a third of what I had seen, of what I had been able to grasp of the art of Europe. But as I thought it over, I realized that what Europe had built over the centuries could not be imitated in a day. Canada would have to grow slowly into this new experience of riding.

Many months later, after performing each night at the Royal Winter Fair in Toronto, I could see what an impact dressage had made on the audience. The public had enjoyed it, many using the word "fascinating" to describe their feelings. All were unanimous in agreeing that it had proved there was another side to riding besides the "thrills and spills." A most original description of my ride appeared in *The Telegram*, written by a sports writer, Frank Jones: "It's like automatic transmission on horseback. . . . he said. "The lights in the Royal Winter Fair arena dim, the crowd is quiet and the announcer introduces Canadian dressage champion Christilot Hanson on her horse Bonheur. A small, poker-straight, unsmiling girl rides into the ring on a big, rangy race horse. What happens then is something quite unique for Canada. . . . The horse seems to glide on cushioned suspension. He trots in slow motion (passage), then slides across the ring in an effortless sideways canter (traversale). He floats to a standstill and then reverses as if on wheels (half pirouette). The horse, changing step constantly, skips across the arena and pirouettes. . . . As the people cheer, Bonheur canters out with Christilot, unsmiling as ever, staring straight ahead."

What people did not realize was that Bonheur and I were blinded by the spotlights. As far as we were concerned, we performed in the pitchdark night. It was hard to smile in the face of nothing.

Most impressed were the cowboys who wanted to know if I had hidden weights in Bonheur's hooves. Upon my explaining that the passage was a natural gait, they said, "How do you teach a horse to do it?" Some RCMP men could not get over the flying changes 4, 3, 2, 1 tempo. "How do you teach this to a horse?" they asked. I felt helpless. How was I to explain a long process of training, so new, so strange to North America, in a few words?

But let me return to the Veranstaltung. Every night after the show was over, the public was allowed to walk through the barns. When they had gone, all show participants converged on the Eden Hotel for supper. Franz Joseph was allowed in by the management, since the place was always heavily patronized by Neindorff students. Standing up before the small, but probably most serious, collection of young dressage riders in the world, der Chef began: "You have done well, but the longeing could have been better." Raging at some, he told all what we could do to improve. We got home at one and fell exhausted into bed. The next morning we were at the stables by 9:30, working our horses. In the afternoon we plaited their manes and got them ready for the evening performance.

That night corks popped once more in the Eden Hotel and champagne frothed over the glasses. Hobbe remarked lightheartedly, "Why worry, we've got loads!" All lady riders received five pink carnations and all gentleman riders a bottle of champagne. Der Chef received a huge bottle of Schnapps. On empty stomachs the bubbles soon took effect! I presented one carnation to Herr von Neindorff which he wore in his buttonhole all evening. In his stall Bonheur wore two on either side of his halter. I had not realized how nervous I had been until we began to let down. Hobbe had ridden the only stallion in the quadrille, and he was so relieved it was all over that he let himself go in a cha-cha with me. The next morning no one had to ride. Herr von Neindorff had declared it a day of rest for man and beast. Needless to say, Franz Joseph walked away the steadiest from the happy party, faithfully following his master back to the barn and the horses which were always foremost among Herr von Neindorff's concerns.

In August the public had its first view of Bonheur as a Grand Prix horse at a show in Wiesenthal. Performing a *kur* (free-style ride) in the middle of a colourful jumping ring before 3,000 spectators, we were loudly cheered. The city's mayor presented me with a large bouquet of roses and a plaque with the town's coat of arms. By this time Bonheur had understood what was wanted in the piaffe, and actually picked up his feet in two-time, for the piaffe is a two-beat movement. The next thing was to develop greater impulsion, and to do it without Herr von Neindorff standing behind us with the whip. Bonheur's extended trot was excellent. His front legs came almost parallel to the ground! This is what Bonheur was admired for in Tokyo.

The time had now come for me to face international competition. The show I was to make my debut in was at Rotterdam. It was held under the auspices of Prince Bernhard of the Netherlands and one competed in it only by invitation. Hobbe took care of that. An official invitation was sent to me after he had brought a Dutch judge to Karlsruhe to see me and Bonheur work.

Because there was to be another Veranstaltung at the same time as the Rotterdam show, Herr von Neindorff wasn't too happy to let me go, especially since he had just tried me on a troublesome horse in the quadrille which had gone perfectly for me. "Now you'll have to stay," he said, knowing full well I couldn't. For there was no turning back now. September 5 was the day of the Grand Prix, the day when 55 per cent of a perfect score had to be achieved, or the Canadian Olympic Equestrian Committee would wait until the next Olympiad.

A private horse-trailer was rented, which was to take Bonheur, a Canadian groom who was specially flown over for the show, and me to Holland. Since I was an international guest of the Rotterdam show, all expenses were paid for me the moment we were within Holland's borders. Reservations were made at the Hilton Hotel. There I met Mother, who had arrived by jet the same day. I still associate the Hilton in Rotterdam with shrimp cocktails, my favourite delicacy: the shrimps were enormous!

In the following days I constantly had to remind Mother not to speak Dutch to me. *"Hoe is het met de piaffe"* were her first words. She seemed nervous. I told her that at his best Bonheur was able to perform the twenty piaffe steps required in the Grand Prix, but that having learned the movement for the first time, he sometimes needed a second urging to do it perfectly. However, when she saw us practising in the ring, Mother relaxed. "He goes beautifully!" she exclaimed.

Although I was nervous also, I felt confident and eager to compete. But it seemed that when one thing went wrong, everything else went wrong with my first venture into Grand Prix competition.

I had received permission to compete in a senior, international show despite my age because I was Canada's official representative in dressage. The Dutch show officials went out of their way to oblige me. Bonheur got an enormous box stall assigned to him. The poor animal had not enjoyed his roomy quarters for a minute when I bumped into Henry Gilhuis, a Dutch acquaintance of mine. Henry asked me to trade Bonheur's larger stall for his very much smaller one, because his horse was badly hurt. What to do? I felt I ought to grant a colleague a justifiable request.

The morning before the test, Bonheur rolled in the small space and banged his hip bone. That evening he would not canter. I did not sleep much that night, nor did my groom. He was up most of the night rubbing alcohol and absorbine on the bruise and overslept in the morning. We were scheduled to go in at 9:30 a.m. I came to Bonheur's stall at 8 o'clock. His braiding had only begun, the groom still yawning. I rushed through the rest of the mane and mounted with still a good half hour left to warm up, or so I thought.

"You have ten minutes, Juffrouw Hanson," the ring steward announced.

"Ten minutes!" I exclaimed. "My watch must have stopped!"

Hobbe, on hand to help, shook his head. "You should always have *two* watches when in competition," he said, graciously offering his advice too late.

"Ten minutes! Mom, where is my hairnet?"

Mother searched frantically in my silk top hat. "I know I put it in here," she said, looking helplessly into the hat, but she could not find the hairnet from sheer nerves. Hobbe searched too and triumphantly picked it out of the same object in which Mother had looked three times.

Then the moment came for me to canter in without warming up, and worse, without knowing whether Bonheur would canter at all.

"What's the matter! Are you cold?" Hobbe asked Mother.

She stood holding her arms and trembling. He put his jacket around her shoulders and accompanied her to the stands, where they sat together. Mother had her Bolex movie camera poised to record the deciding event for those back in Canada.

Bonheur appeared through the trees at a walk, coming into the grounds. I sat solemnly straight and I prayed with all my might as I waited for the bell. Bonheur's coat glistened in the early morning sun. Mother wished she had never promised to film the event. Hobbe sat back and looked grave.

The bell rang, Mother started her Bolex, and Bonheur broke stiffly into a canter. Down the centre line, two feet on either side, the horse moved straight, halting at X for the salute. The Bolex stopped whirring, its operator overwhelmed by the noise it made against the hushed silence of the crowd. Only moments before, during other rides, a blacksmith's hammer had clinked in the background, the stands had been noisy with talking and coughing. Now only the patter of hooves could be heard, springing off the moist sand.

At the end of the test I again returned to X for the salute. As my hand came to my side and my head bowed, the stands burst into an ovation. The piaffe had gone haywire, and the transitions had not been good, but the over-all picture had been "concentrated elegance," I was told.

Baroness von Spiegel, who had seen me train in Hannover with the General, came running to me while I was dismounting. *"Das war eine grosze Leistung!* (That was a great accomplishment!)" she said. Later I was interviewed by World Radio. The announcer asked me, "Were you disappointed with your seventh-place showing?"

"No," I answered. "I came here to qualify for Tokyo and I achieved over the required 55 per cent in my marks."

Later in the afternoon we performed again for the public. Bonheur, excited by the band and the huge crowd, did close to 50 one-tempo flying changes in a row.

"What do you think?" I asked Mother back in the hotel room, while we both packed to go off in different directions, she to Toronto, I to Karlsruhe.

"To my mind it was a victory," Mother said. "You competed with experienced horses and riders. Unfortunate circumstances and all, you and Bonheur didn't look out of place. You've improved tremendously since I saw you last. It's a difference of day and night. Hobbe said so too."

I sighed, relieved. Coming from Mother, it meant a great deal.

7) Tokyo 1964!

Bonheur was finally booked to fly to Tokyo from Stuttgart on September 30. I would follow him two days later. He was fed bran mashes and only jogged the last few days before the trip, so that he would be relaxed. I rushed around madly, trying to pack his gear, wash his bandages and get all his papers straight.

On the morning of Bonheur's departure a government veterinarian arrived to look at him, then watched approvingly as two stable boys washed his legs and feet thoroughly in disinfectant. This was to keep him germ-free until he reached Tokyo.

At last all was packed. My black trunk, which was to accompany Bonheur, was filled to capacity. Three people had to stand on it to close it. Wolfgang turned up with his trailer at five p.m. and Bonheur, decked out in a Canadian team blanket, a hood, four bandages and bell boots, started the first leg of a long-to-be-remembered journey. Herr von Neindorff's last words to him were: *"Macht's gut!"* He gave me two dozen carrots to make the trip a little sweeter for my horse.

The two-hour drive to Stuttgart passed in reminiscence.

99

At the airport we found the Pan American officials waiting for their precious cargo. There were also the inevitable newspaper people. As soon as the car stopped, two reporters opened the door and immediately started to fire questions at the rate of fifty a minute. "How are your chances? How old are you? How old is the horse? Are you nervous? What do you think of the Beatles? Can we take pictures? Do you believe the Germans will win?"

I didn't know what my chances were, I was seventeen years old (I told the truth), the horse was nine, yes, I was very nervous, upset . . . and I wished they would all go away! I didn't care for the Beatles, they would take pictures even if I said not to! I couldn't say if the Germans were going to win or not. My only concern was to get the horse on the plane in one piece and have him arrive in Tokyo in the same condition.

We had two hours until take-off time, for the Jet Cargo Clipper was behind schedule. At last the machine arrived. Wolfgang helped unload the horse and led him straight into his flying-box. It had been specially built for Bonheur in Germany and was wide enough for him. It was padded all around with foam rubber. The floor was covered with sawdust. The front, which was also padded to keep his lovely coat from being scratched, was built so that he could look out. The box was on a hydraulic lift, and when Bonheur was safely in the box, the tractor pulled him across the airfield to the side of the jet.

It was dark by this time. I prayed Bonny would keep his nerves as he heard the scream of planes taking off on his right, and saw the huge, metallic bird with lights blinking toward which he was being propelled. All during this period the reporters never stopped asking questions. They didn't help the situation by continually popping flash bulbs at the poor horse's head.

The attendants jockeyed the lift around to the side of the plane, pushed the button, and the platform started to go up. For a horse, this must be a nerve-racking moment. He watches the ground disappear from beneath him and the huge hole above approach. When Bonheur reached the same level as the plane, the attendants pushed the box into the aircraft and at that moment another plane, taking off, literally skimmed the top of the attendants' heads. Bonheur ducked instinctively, but did nothing more than get a pained look in his eyes. They rolled the box to the back of the machine and fastened it down well. I could breathe easily once more, for at last my horse had reached the plane without mishap. I went inside and made sure that he was comfortably installed with plenty of food and water. Special ropes and webbing were put over loose boxes and trunks, for cargo has a nasty habit of floating around when planes hit air-pockets and drop several hundred feet.

The reporters finally disappeared with their bounty, and the time was nearing when I too would have to leave the plane and trust that Bonheur and I would be reunited in Tokyo. Suddenly I realized that Wolfgang was missing. As I looked out the door through which Bonheur had just come, the wild idea crossed my mind that maybe Wolfgang had fallen out. No such thing. Mr. Keil was sitting in the pilot's chair, completely engrossed in the panels of knobs and levers, charts and radar equipment.

The time came to leave. I kissed Bonheur goodbye, gave him a carrot and told him to arrive safe and sound. As I left, he perked his ears and whinnied softly and I felt as if I were letting him down. His trusting gaze followed me out of the doorway. I knew what the next three days could hold for him.

The pilot of the plane had promised to radio a safe take-off immediately. An indescribable feeling of helplessness took hold of me, as I stood and watched the giant silver plane scream past with the most precious possession I had. The plane rocked back on its tail and climbed steeply. The moment had come when many horses have to be killed, because the noise drives them mad or the acceleration throws them back on their tails and they panic. I tortured myself for the next few minutes with images of Bonheur falling down in his box, injuring himself, and being shot. Then a voice crackled through the speaker: "All O.K. Horse fine, we're on our way! Roger."

Wolfgang helped me into my coat and we walked out into the chilly night air. I felt like a wrung-out sponge. It was two o'clock in the morning when I reached bed and fell asleep with the image of Bonheur en route to Tokyo, en route at last to the Olympics!

The next morning the doctor administered to me a second vaccine shot against cholera. Japan had recently had an epidemic and had requested all Olympic contestants and spectators to be immunized against it. Given in the chest below the collarbone, the shot became quite sore and any arm movement was a painful process. Fever and sleepiness descended upon me for the rest of the day.

I was scheduled to leave Frankfurt for Paris at seven in the evening, October 2. From Paris I would fly straight to Tokyo. On my last night in Karlsruhe Herr von Neindorff asked me out to dinner and gave me his last-minute instructions. He had prepared a day-to-day plan of how to bring Bonheur to his peak gradually, giving him at least six days with no hard work to recover from the gruelling trip. He also cautioned me to work early in the morning, as far from curious eyes as possible, so that I would be less likely to become nervous. I will never forget his counsel that night as he spoke of the higher ideals of riding. He warned me not to judge my riding by the percentage of marks I received, but to set myself the highest standard I possibly could. He told me how he had often won and been unhappy with the ride from his own idealistic point of view, and how often he had lost and been completely satisfied with his performance. He stressed that I was laying the foundation for the future. I was building my reputation, gaining daily in experience. At seventeen I should be thrilled to have reached Grand Prix level at all. I knew that he was the greatest riding teacher in the world, and I felt humbly grateful when he offered me the chance to come back and work in the Institute as his assistant. I hoped I would be able to return, but if I didn't, I knew that the time I had spent learning from him would stand out in later years as one of my richest experiences.

The morning and the afternoon were spent packing my own belongings. And what a chore it was! Wolfgang's deadline had been 6 o'clock, and at 5 I was still packing, always finding more and not even bathed or changed.

"Toot! Toot!" I looked out of the window to find Wolfgang looking up, watch in hand. "Come up and help me pack!" I called down.

"Pack!" he gasped, and all colour ran from his face. "You mean you're not packed?"

"I am almost," I said. With Wolfgang doing an Indian war dance on my suitcases, they finally shut.

"I only hope customs don't open them," was his modest prayer.

And so with three suitcases and three handbags, filled with odds and ends such as books and vitamin pills for Bonheur, I made my final exit from the old house. Frau Kuhs wished me luck and gave me some candies to keep me from starving on the way to the Frankfurt airport.

Next stop was the Reitinstitut, where farewells were said to all personnel, to Kaiser Franz and Jarvado in particular, and then to Herr von Neindorff, who was in the only place he could possibly have been—the riding ring, on a horse. I left him a box of cigars and a bunch of carrots for my "boys" and sadly said goodbye to a place that had become very dear to me. It was hard to imagine that I wouldn't be back there the next morning. Although Herr von Neindorff and I shook hands cheerfully, there was a funny feeling that we had become better friends than we had realized. I promised to write and invited him to come and visit Canada. Had it not been for the wonderful help I had received from der Chef, Wolfgang, and many others during my stay in Karlsruhe, I could never look back at this period of my life with such warm feelings. I made up my mind, if ever the occasion should arise, to be a good hostess to them and show them my city and my country.

At the Frankfurt airport my baggage was found to be considerably over the weight limit, so I arranged to send the bulk of it by air cargo. My flight number was called and Wolfgang added to my various purses, bags and umbrella with a large bunch of dark pink carnations. Trying to balance everything while opening my purse to extract my passport was not the easiest task. But finally, after many touch-and-go moments, I made it onto the plane.

Orly Airport outside Paris was reached within an hour. At the terminal, Air France gave me a ticket for the bus into

Paris, francs for the taxi and papers to claim a reserved room at the Hotel Claridge. At the check-in desk the hotel clerk informed me that Air France had reserved two rooms, but that I was the third Air France passenger to turn up. In other words, there was no room available. Paris was at the height of her convention season, and there was not a room to be found anywhere. I showed him my papers entitling me to a room. After a hurried call to the airline he said he could give me a bathroom to stay in.

I was led up the stairs to a huge bathroom with a bed in it, and dresses and suits and shoes all over. It looked very occupied. The clerk made small work of collecting all the clothes and shoes and without further ado threw them into the hallway. He brought in fresh towels, told me to lock my door, gave me the key, and added that breakfast would be brought up at six in the morning. Wishing me a good night, he left abruptly.

I ran some cold water in the bathtub and let my drooping carnations float in it. I got undressed, washed my face, and lay down to catch some sleep. I had been in bed about ten minutes when I heard the doorknob turn, then rattle vehemently. I sat up, terrified, but then I heard steps recede down the hallway. It finally dawned on me that since I was in a public bathroom, many people would not realize that someone was spending the night there. At different intervals during the rest of the night, people would shake the door knob, rattle it, mutter in French and go away to find a more yielding bathroom door.

Morning came quickly, and with it a breakfast of hot rolls with butter and jam, and a pot of delicious coffee and hot milk. At 6:30 I was ready to leave for the airport again. The carnations, however, could not accompany me any further.

I settled down in an airport waiting room with the words "Paris—Tokyo" over the door. One of my fellow passengers caught my attention immediately. He was small, dark and had a familiar face. I tried to recollect where I had seen him before. Then I remembered. Rotterdam! It was Nelson Pessoa, the leading Brazilian jumping rider. From Pony Club days onward, I had looked up to the great international stars, never dreaming of meeting them face to face. I wanted to have his autograph, but didn't know how to go about it. Finally I gathered courage, walked over to him and asked for it. He said that I too looked rather familiar, but he could not place me. I mentioned Rotterdam and before long we were deep in technical discussions. Once on board the big jet, we continued our conversation.

I had booked a direct flight to Tokyo over the Pole, or so I thought. But the voice of the captain startled me as he announced we would land in Madrid in an hour's time! I was on the wrong plane. The destination was the same, however, only we were going the long way around. At the Madrid airport the whole Spanish field hockey team boarded the plane with an astounding number of officials and delegates.

Once more on our way, everyone settled down to reading or writing, everyone, that is, but the members of the Spanish team. They spent their time playing noisy card games, drinking gaily and worrying every girl that dared to walk down the aisle to the rear of the plane. The stewardesses had to be very calm and patient to put up with it all. The rest of the flight went off normally, however, with occasional landings at places like Teheran, Calcutta and Bangkok.

Finally the long-awaited words were heard: "One hour to Tokyo." Everyone started to straighten up and pack books away. I decided to risk a short walk to the back of the plane to comb my hair.

Everyone watched with awe as the night lights of the huge city of Tokyo came into view. Excitement mounted, and when the plane landed pandemonium broke loose. A great Hurrah! came from the Spanish team. They shook hands solemnly and, much to the stewardesses' dismay, began dashing from window to window. I caught the excitement, as did Pessoa. Before the plane had stopped rolling we were all up and gathering belongings. The pilot lurched to a stop rather suddenly and the whole mob flew to the front of the plane, landing in one happy heap. But order was finally restored and we all got off.

The Spaniards were met by an official of their delegation. Nelson Pessoa was met by the Brazilian officials, and as I looked around with a feeling of mounting desperation, a tall gentleman walked up to me and introduced himself as the Canadian attaché. I was so relieved to have been claimed!

And this was Japan! The crowds in the visitors' areas were enormous. I was told that they were waiting to see foreign athletes arrive. For the next three weeks I was constantly surprised at the interest shown by the Japanese people in the Olympics. Being an Olympic participant, I did not have too much trouble getting through customs. I thanked heaven that they did not open my overstuffed suitcases. The Spaniards boarded a bus to take them to the Olympic Village. The Brazilians went in a small foreign auto, and we drove out in a white Jaguar XK 120. I was very tired, but still had enough life left in me to see that we were, to my way of thinking, driving on the wrong side of the road. Besides this alarming discovery, there seemed to be no passing lane, as cars scooted by on the inside and on the outside. One enterprising taxi driver even went so far as to drive on the sidewalk to get past another car.

Finally we arrived at Olympic Village, called Yoyogi Village by the Japanese. The flags of all the participating nations were fluttering in front of the administrative offices. Floodlights lit the area, and here again crowds of Japanese were observing curiously all the occupants arriving in cars and buses.

Once we were in the building, I was given all kinds of identification papers and badges. These would enable me to get past the numerous guards who were stationed in front of all gates and entrances leading into the Village. Every team member was also given a railway pass and a bus pass, providing him with free transportation in the city and surrounding areas. The Japanese had planned everything down to the smallest detail. We were even equipped with a small white card, which we were to give to a passerby if we found ourselves lost somewhere in the sprawling city of Tokyo. In Japanese, it asked the reader to phone the number on the card, and an Olympic taxi would be sent immediately to pick up the visitor and bring him safely back to the Village.

When the registration was finished, we drove into the Village and stopped in front of another gate. The attaché told me that this was the entrance to the women's quarters and that he had no permission to set foot inside it. Doctors were the only men who could enter this forbidden territory legally. One of the Japanese attendants went to fetch the Canadian girls' chaperone, who helped me carry my bags up to the room in which I was to stay.

We opened the door quietly and tip-toed inside. The sound of heavy breathing, sighs and occasional coughing broke the silence. The chaperone informed me that my three roommates were members of the swim team. After wishing me a good night, she crept stealthily out of the room, stopping to warn me to be as quiet as possible and try not to wake the others up. I promptly stumbled over a large cardboard box on my way to the shower room.

The next day dawned bright and clear, and by 8 o'clock the three girls were trying to move about the room without waking the newcomer. After three books had hit the floor and one glass of water had been spilled, I gave up any notion of sleeping and sat up. We all introduced ourselves. Soon I was catching up on bits of news and information concerning the Games and the Village. Carol Anne Morrow, the diver, and Jane Hughes had to go to practice early. Barbara Hounsell had been given the day off because of her cough and she offered to show me around the Village. After going through the box of team clothing, some of which fitted perfectly and some . . . well, not so perfectly, I found a collection of gold and coloured maple leaf pins. Enquiring why I needed such a number of pins, I was told of a custom that had grown up with the Olympics. Everyone traded pins. I would give one of mine to an athlete of another country in exchange for one of his. By the time I went home my blazer was covered with pins of different nations.

After Barbara and I had got dressed in our team sweaters and stuck a few of our Canadian pins on our lapels, we left for a tour of the Village. Our first stop was at one of the many dining halls scattered throughout the place. We headed for the table where some men in red and white jackets with CANADA stencilled across the back were sitting. I was introduced to two of the members of our gymnastic team. A couple of Australian field hockey players joined the table and then my long-lost Spanish friends from the plane descended upon us. It was a happy meal. The air was filled with the laughter and talk of many nations, all as different as the foods we ate. Many of the Asiatic athletes started the day with a bowl of soup and a plate of rice. As for me, I settled for the customary fruit juice, toast and jam and coffee. I also started collecting apples from the table, with Bonheur in mind.

I often marvelled at the way athletes could talk to one another. One asked in Spanish, the other answered in English, and both understood. A Frenchman, upon hearing I was a dressage rider, informed me that one of the members of the Jury was the French General Margot. "*Il est très méchant!* (He is very naughty!)" he added. It appeared that the eighty-year-old general held the opinion that amazons belong in the park, not in competition with men. (Oh! la la!) I thought to myself that General von Oppeln would agree with that. He always used to ask every man he met at cocktail parties in Canada: "Do you ride?" Mostly the answer was, "No, but my wife does," whereupon the General muttered, "Always 'the wife' in North America!" He used to boast that Germany was still a "man's country," where men, not women, were the leaders. To these views I added my two cents' worth. Dressage, being an art, ought to be represented by men and women alike, as music is. The question then arises whether it would be desirable to split up the competition and have men compete against men, and women with women, as in gymnastics. I personally don't think so. If dressage were a purely physical matter, this would indeed seem the right answer, but since the intellectual and spiritual aspects of dressage exceed the physical by far, women are as qualified for dressage as men.

Back in our room once more, Barbara had to take her medicine and I settled down to write some letters and wait for the phone call that would tell me Bonheur had arrived at the airport. The Pan Am officials had promised to let me know as soon as the plane landed. But there was no news all day. After I was told at lunch that four horses had been shot on the way to Tokyo, my anxiety began to mount.

In the meantime, getting used to the lay-out of the Village, I noticed bicycles were to be found in front of all main buildings. Seeing a few athletes use them, I enquired whether or not I too could use one to save myself the long walk to the dining hall. The Japanese interpreter assured me that they were there exactly for that purpose. Upon arriving at my destination, I should just leave my bicycle there for someone else who would want to travel in some other direction. The only catch was that on finishing a meal, there was invariably not a bike in sight.

The boys had found the perfect answer to this problem. A girl would start walking, disappointed at not having found a bike. A luckier male athlete would soon come blithely up the road. The bell would ring incessantly and then he would pull up beside the girl. In French, Spanish, German, Russian, or some invented language, he would motion to her to sit on the cross-bars of his bike, offering to pedal her to her destination. If the offer was accepted, the hair-raising ride would begin, weaving and wobbling all over the road, or going faster and faster until the only thing one could hear were the damsel's frantic screams.

Another favourite trick was to pedal right by the place where the girl had planned to get off, oblivious to her pointing and yelling. Having reached his living quarters, the fellow would pedal in circles, ringing the bell until his fellow teammates came to the windows to admire his kidnapped bounty. Satisfied, he'd then pedal back to the original destination, drop the girl off, thank her profusely and pedal away to find another unsuspecting soul.

A few days of living in Japan convinced me that every Japanese must own a camera. Spectators were allowed to roam about the Village during certain hours, and their fondest dream was to be photographed with some athlete. Any athlete there soon became immune to the battery of cameras that confronted him at every moment, on a bicycle, buying stamps, drinking a Coke, or with a mouth full of rice.

At 6 o'clock in the evening of my second day in Japan, the Canadian girls' chaperone ran excitedly into my room. "He's here!" she cried.

"Where? When? How is he?" I babbled.

"They made some mistake! He arrived early this morning and he's up at the Equestrian Park already."

"He's been here for a whole day and now I find out!" I pulled my clothes on and reached for my purse. I was shown the platform where the buses left and the schedule of arrivals and departures. I missed the scenery completely on my first ride up to Baji-Koen (Equestrian Park). The prospect of seeing my horse and Emily Brown, my Pony Club pal who had been chosen as Bonheur's Olympic attendant, was too exciting.

When I arrived I asked at the information office which barn Bonheur was in. The superintendent motioned to the No. 1 barn, one of the five shed rows built of concrete block. There were ropes all around this barn and a big sign reading "Quarantine Area. No unauthorized person may enter." Authorized or not, I intended to see my horse and I ducked under the ropes. Inside the dark building, the smell of disinfectant was strong. Right inside the door were two bowls filled with strong antiseptic in which every one was supposed to wash his hands.

I heard the familiar crunching of hay. Having finally located the light switch, I made my way up the aisle of empty stalls until I found the one that housed my horse. His head was low, his coat dusty, his lovely eyes were listless·

"Hey Bonny," I called softly. His ears pricked up and his nostrils began to quiver as he breathed in. His muzzle in my hand, he sniffed eagerly, then went over my whole body, sniffing, sniffing, sniffing. With a great sigh he rubbed his head up and down my back. As long as he could do that, he was still alright!

On closer examination I saw he had lost weight, but otherwise he did not have a scratch on him. After checking his hay and water supplies, I wished him goodnight and went off to find Emily. I looked in at the Equestrian Park dining room. There I saw the back view of a familiar figure. Emily was just finishing supper. From the droop of her shoulders I saw how tired she was. Even her pony tail hung limply!

I nudged her in the ribs. "Hi stranger!"

Emily whirled around. "Christy! You are a welcome sight! Here sit down. Do you want a cup of coffee?" Emily is one of those people who consider coffee an essential item in life, more so than food. We sat down and laughed happily as we recounted the wild experiences of our journeys to Japan.

It appeared that Bonheur had been travelling with "Bold Minstrel," an American three-day horse who had been sent to replace "Markham," who had panicked in the plane and been shot. Bold Minstrel was accompanied by his owner-attendant Bill Haggard, but Emily had ended up looking after both horses as Bill slept and ate most of the time. When they landed in Tokyo there was no one to meet them, "And there," said Emily, "the picnic ended. Bill was really upset because American Express didn't meet him, and I wondered where you were. We finally got the horses loaded into the van. There was only one man at the airport who spoke English and he was so busy that we had to communicate with the natives with sign language and exasperated looks. It took a lot of sweat and tears to get those horses onto the van without a scratch. Then came the death-defying dash through Tokyo with our silent driver."

Honking constantly, the driver tore through the city, narrowly missing three-wheeled trucks, very large and very small foreign cars, women carrying their children papoose-style and old men trotting across the street waving yellow flags. After three quarters of an hour of this, he made a sudden U-turn in the middle of a busy street and sped back the way they had come. Having no means of communication with their insane driver, Emily and Bill merely continued shaking and hoped for the best. It turned out that the driver had missed the street he should have taken. Anyway, they arrived safe but not quite sound at Baji-Koen. Since Bold Minstrel was a three-day horse, he had to stay on the van for the 90-mile trip to the three-day site. "You don't know how I felt," Emily said, "when after unloading Bonheur I heard the van race down the road, taking with it the only familiar face in Japan. I haven't heard whether or not they made it. . . ."

It was all so comical I couldn't help laughing and I urged Emily to continue her story. "After a long wait," she recalled, "Bonheur and I were allowed to come inside the stable yard where the quarantine men poked, pried and peered at the poor horse and chattered away to themselves. Finally I could put Bonheur in the cement-block stable and take his bandages off, but I was not permitted to exercise him until tomorrow. I tried to make him as comfortable as possible though, rubbing him all over with absorbine. He loved it, he was so stiff. The Japanese gave me some hand-tied bundles of nice, soft rice straw, musty hay and clean whole oats. I was feeling a bit lost by then, so I cleaned his halter, bandages and pails, arranged the tack room and hoped for you to come along. But nothing happened, except that the vets checked Bonheur all over, took blood tests, gave him needles and asked a lot of questions in Japanese. Finally they left and I massaged him again, fed him, then grabbed my 1,000-pound suitcase and staggered up to where I thought I was to stay. Guess what! Nobody spoke English. After some more sign language someone got a book and pointed to the phrase, 'Please wait one moment while I get an interpreter,' which was written in seven different languages. Finally I was shown to an empty room that had the Canadian flag stuck on the door. By this time my sleepiness had worn off and I decided to have something to eat. So I was half through my dinner when my luck changed and you walked in."

Em found that I had had my problems too. She laughed hearing about my sleeping in a bathroom in the Paris hotel and taking the wrong plane to Tokyo. We agreed about getting organized the next day and hoped things would go smoother from here on in. I ran to catch the last bus of the night that was getting ready to drive back to the Village. The trip back was far more enjoyable for me. At last I knew Bonheur was safe. He would get the best treatment possible from Emily.

The next morning I pulled on my riding breeches for the first time in a week and hurriedly grabbed a bike to get down to the bus terminal. I coasted happily down the hill, a bag filled with apples swinging back and forth on the handle bars.

Suddenly a fellow in the red and yellow sweat shirt of the Spanish team appeared in my path. My legs pedalled backwards, my hands worked the brakes—and still I continued to pick up speed. Horrified, I didn't even think of using the bell or screaming. The inevitable happened.

We lay in a heap, surrounded by apples. We were both shocked to death. I saw the tire mark imprinted on the back of the boy's sweat shirt. Thankfully, however, he wasn't hurt. Dazed by the impact and the spectacle of the apples surrounding him, he got up and anxiously asked if I was alright.

Since no harm was done, we exchanged pins and continued on our respective ways, he shaking his head in disbelief. I made special efforts from this time on to drive on the right side of the road, which was the left.

Once more at Baji-Koen, Emily and I took turns walking Bonheur up and down the lane leading to the track and exercise arenas. Bonheur squealed and kicked up his heels, proving that he was recuperating fast from the journey. We then started working in our tack stall, while Bonheur got some hay to munch on. We had done this often at Pony Club rallies. To do it again at the Olympics we found hilarious!

In the course of the afternoon, the Italian horses were brought in to occupy the stalls beside Bonheur. From then on the place was never quite the same. When Bonheur had been walked for the second time that day, Emily brought him out on the stable floor to groom him and rub his legs. I was in the tack room cleaning one of his bridles. Before long I heard a desperate call for help, and opening the door, found the whole Italian team laughing and making eyes at Emily as she tried to do her work. Under the battery of critical eyes, Emily fumbled nervously.

It did not take the Italians long to decide that two helpless little girls were working beside them. They would not leave us alone. On seeing me put a bandage on, one of them, Amerigo, threw his hands in the air, tore the bandage off, and started all over again. Another insisted on grooming Bonheur Italian style. Emily reached her limit one day when the soap sponge with which she had been cleaning the saddle was grabbed out of her hand and alcohol poured on it. She snatched it back: "Please! I'd rather do it myself!"

"*Mama mia!*" gasped the well-meaning Italian at so much feminine independence. Then he looked heavenward and made a cross, as if saying: "I wash my hands in innocence."

When we moved out of quarantine we were assigned Barn No. 4, with the Germans and Russians as our neighbours. Each team had its own group of officials, the Russians even having their own blacksmith with them. Looking at Bonheur's feet, the Russian blacksmith was of the opinion that his shoes were too heavy. He wanted to put Russian shoes on Bonheur. When I objected that to change my horse's shoes would hurt his performance, he presented me with a set of Russian shoes to use in Canada.

In the meantime I had met Inez Fischer Credo from Vancouver, the other Canadian representative in dressage, and Dr. Sargeant, the Canadian *chef d'équipe*, who were staying in a hotel outside the Village. One afternoon we bumped into each other on the exercise grounds, and Inez enthused about the Russian riders. "The Germans are good," she said, being herself born and trained in dressage in Germany, "but the Russians are better."

For the next few days I exercised Bonheur only lightly. He was becoming acclimatized nicely. I was usually completely alone as I worked Bonheur according to the instructions of Herr von Neindorff at 5:30 a.m. Bonheur enjoyed the early morning walks around the beautiful Japanese race course, and I had time to admire the artistic landscaping and tree shaping for which the Japanese are famous. Finishing early before the other riders began enabled me to have a relaxing breakfast and then go out and watch the best of the riding world practising. There were the dressage artists Filatov and Neckermann, and the jumpers D'Oriola, Schockemoehle and the world-famous D'Inzeo brothers. What I learned from just watching these great ones is inestimable.

On October 10, the Canadian team donned their parade dresses and blue blazers for the official opening of the Games. We met at Canadian Headquarters and there boarded the buses that would take us to the National Stadium. Along the route to the stadium crowds jammed the sidewalks, cheering and waving flags, and we were soon all leaning out the windows, waving back. The buses halted about an eighth of a mile outside the stadium. We got out, formed in columns, and began the traditional march. By the time the team reached the entrance gates, one of the coaches had managed to get us into something resembling marching order. We entered the stadium. March music was playing. We passed the Emperor's box, where we all turned our heads right, the men taking off their hats. The flag-bearer lowered the flag from a vertical to a horizontal position.

It was a long walk around the cinder track, especially for the girls in their high-heeled parade shoes. As soon as we had lined up on the infield, facing the Emperor, the shoes came off. It took my feet three months to heal. The blood-blisters kept opening. However, at the time I wasn't aware of my feet hurting, for it was really a thrill to see all the other teams come marching in, all in distinctive national dress. Some of the African nations wore tribal robes.

After all the teams were lined up we heard two speeches, by the president of the Organizing Committee and the president of the International Olympic Committee. The speeches were flashed across the scoreboard in English and French. The Emperor then declared the Games open and a fanfare of trumpets sounded.

The Olympic flag made its entrance, carried by eight members of the Japanese Navy. As it was hoisted a huge chorus began singing the Olympic anthem. Following this the mayor of Rome, where the previous Olympics had been held, entered the stadium and presented a commemorative flag to the Governor of Tokyo. There was a booming salute of guns and 10,000 balloons were released on all sides of the stadium.

At last the long-awaited moment arrived. From the northern entrance, the final Olympic torch-runner entered the stadium. All was hushed as he ran up the sixty steps of the back stand and lighted the Sacred Olympic Fire. The chorus broke into the Tokyo Olympic Games' song. This was decidely the high point of the ceremony for the athletes, as they looked up at that flame, thinking of what it stood for. The words of Baron Pierre de Coubertin, that the important thing in the Olympics is not to win, but to participate in the Games, until finally a high world culture is attained, were on the minds of all.

Japan's gymnastic star Takashi Ono took the Olympic oath for all of us: "In the name of all competitors I promise that we will take part in these Olympic Games respecting and abiding by the rules which govern them, in the true spirit of sportsmanship, for the glory of sport and the honour of our teams."

Suddenly the stadium was filled with 8,000 doves that had

been released from cages under the front stands. As we stood gazing heavenward at the grand spectacle, quite a number of spectators and athletes were quickly brought back to reality, for the droppings landed without respect to race, creed or colour.

The Japanese National Anthem was played once more and then five jet planes flew overhead, their vapour trails forming the five Olympic circles perfectly. The Emperor left the stadium, and the athletes marched out to the accompaniment of fireworks. Altogether it was a most thrilling and memorable day.

The opening ceremony marked the end of Bonheur's period of acclimatization. The next twelve days would be spent in intensive training and practising.

Mother arrived a week before competition day. Thanks to the fact that everyone, including the officials, was very busy, I arranged to smuggle her into Baji-Koen. I met her at the airport. I had brought my Canadian blazer with me, and she put it on immediately. I had wanted to take her to the Village, but she insisted I take her to where Bonheur was stabled. We passed easily through customs. No one asked to see her passes. At Baji-Koen, Mother still wearing the blazer, we just marched into Emily's room. Mother stayed as a second attendant. Since there were still two spare beds, Inez and I also moved into the room the following day. I managed to get Mother the correct passes later in the week, but we remained very proud of our little bluff.

Emily, Mother and I would be up every morning at five, but since Inez' horse, "Gordina," did not like to get up early in the morning, Inez worked her later in the day. Emily fed Bonheur, stumbling into the still darkened barn over the bodies of the Mexican grooms who slept in the aisle between their horses' stalls. Often, the only other person awake was the Russian guard, who was there for the same reasons as the Mexicans: to guard against foul play, and to watch in case a horse should get sick during the night. Herr von Neindorff too had insisted upon someone sleeping in front of Bonheur's stall all during the Games. But since Emily was a girl . . . and since so many grooms of different nations were obviously doing a splendid job, we trusted nothing would happen to Bonheur.

We would use one of the numerous rings, or, if it was raining, would go over to the beautiful indoor riding hall. Although it entailed a lot of extra work, it was worth it. I rode to my heart's content, with no outside interference, until one day a husky-looking blonde young man came along. Although I never learned his name, I recognized him as one of the members of the Russian team. He watched engrossed and was back the next morning. Since Bonheur was going exceptionally well, I kept on working. The Russian was soon gesticulating fiercely, motioning to me where I should bend the horse a few degrees more, indicating that I should keep my head up, or signalling that all was well.

Another morning a Japanese general who was to represent his country in dressage crossed our path. "*O hayo gozaimas* (Good morning)," said Mother. The General, pleased at hearing his own language spoken, stopped his horse to have a little talk with her. "Japan is only beginning with dressage," he said. "So is Canada," Mother replied, whereupon the General remarked, "Oh no! Look at the extension of that Canadian horse."

Towards dusk, Bonheur and I would wander off once more, sometimes just to walk, other times to practise certain movements that I felt needed polishing. On a red-letter day for me, Filatov, the Russian gold medal winner at Rome, was pedalling around the exercise area late in the afternoon. He joined the big, blonde Russian who was already standing watching me practise. An animated talk between the two in Russian followed.

Russia's first dressage rider praised Bonheur's two-track work, his extended paces, and flying changes. He gave me some very good tips on improving his walk and executing more exact pirouettes. Then came the subject I had been dreading silently: "Passage! Passage!" cried Filatov, the unsurpassed master in that particular high school movement. I tried to look innocent. Hoping to get out of it, I asked with grim humour: *"Passage? Was ist das?* (Passage? What is that?) "

"Was ist das?" roared Filatov, slapping his thighs and laughing. Turning to the bystanders, he repeated: *"Was ist das? Was ist das? Das ist gut!"*

The idea of asking what a passage was three days before riding the Grand Prix in the Olympics hit him square in the funny bone. Nevertheless, he pressed and pressed until I was forced to show him the passage. He raised his eyebrows in pleased surprise, then dropped his bicycle and joined me in the ring. Helping me to collect Bonheur even more from the ground, he gave me many more useful tips and the next day showed me on his stallion "Absent" the Russian method of teaching the piaffe. This in itself was worth the trip to Tokyo. I was also pleased to see that Filatov liked Bonheur. He let it be known that he wanted to ride him, and so we set a date for the day after the Grand Prix, since international rules forbid anyone other than the rider who is to present the horse to mount him before competition.

Against all expectations Bonheur put on weight in Japan,

because of the good-quality oats and hay in that country. He was perky, hungry and acted like a two-year-old. He seemed to get twice as much out of a quart of grain in Tokyo as out of a gallon of German oats. As a matter of fact, he became so fresh that Emily and I had to cut down his food.

Excitement mounted as the day drew near. If I hadn't had so much work to do, the nervous strain would probably have driven me out of my mind.

The night before the competition I groomed Bonheur especially well, washing his legs, mane and tail. Emily gave the saddle and bridle a superb cleaning and polished the minute buckles on the bridle. The Russians thought she had gone crazy, sticking a matchstick through the little holes in the bridle strap.

On the morning of the great day I experienced the panic that many athletes do. I didn't want to get up, feeling that maybe if I didn't, I wouldn't have to face the day. Emily soon dispelled all such notions from my head. At 5:30 she pulled all the bedclothes off me, and told me to stop stalling and get up!

The jitters soon left me when I started out on an early morning walk with Bonheur. He was scheduled to enter the ring at approximately 10:30, being the eighth horse in. I decided that I should walk him for half an hour before breakfast. While I was walking, Emily went to have her breakfast, so that upon her return she could start right away on the final grooming and polishing.

After the walk I tried to eat something and changed into my good white breeches and shirt. Throwing an old sweater on, I then headed back to the barn to braid Bonheur's mane. We had decided that since I had always done his mane, I would be able to do the best job. This was a Godsend, for while concentrating on doing a good job it was impossible for me to work up nerves. Having finished braiding at 8, we left Bonheur for an hour's rest. For some reason, after being polished and braided and fiddled with, he needs at least an hour to settle down and relax. I had learned early in his show career that if I rushed or pushed him in any way, he would come out peevish as a prima donna. I also took the time to rest and to look over my Grand Prix test, which I had learned by heart many months ago.

An hour and a half before starting time I was tacked up and ready to start walking around the warm-up area. Bonheur had always needed a generous amount of work before showing at his best. After half an hour of walking, I slowly began to loosen him up for the test to come. We heard the thunderous applause as Filatov entered the arena, and again as he made his exit. "He's in the lead again," I thought.

The time grew closer. Bonheur was warming up fast and going well. Emily sprayed him all over with an anti-fly preparation and brushed his hooves once move. Mother helped me into the black cut-away coat and handed me the black cylinder hat.

Ten minutes to go. . . . I pulled on my white leather gloves, as Emily ran a cloth over the horse to pick up any dust. She quickly oiled his hooves and then said: "You're on your own."

I mounted Bonheur. We walked and jogged around as one of the Swedish horses went through the last movements of the test. There was the familiar dryness in my mouth, and the sudden feverish heat hit me as the Japanese gatesman signalled me into the fenced-in area, where the dressage ring had been set up. I went in, and immediately noticed the change in ground. It was soft and rather spongy from the rain (we had struck the west monsoon in Japan), and it sort of sucked at the horse's feet. I knew I would have to watch certain movements because of the possibility of slipping. A light drizzle of rain began to come down.

Over the loudspeaker my name and number and country were announced in French, Japanese, English and German. Then the fateful little bell rang, signalling me to begin my ride.

The next twelve minutes were indescribable. I lost consciousness of everything around me. I was alone with my horse, going through the most difficult dressage test in the world. The stillness, the communication between the two of us, as I asked for the different movements, and as he gave; an extra pressure, a silent rebuke, an unseen praising, a firm correction; all these passed between us as though through telegraph wires. In the piaffe I sensed the difficulty Bonheur was having to pull his feet out of the very soft footing. As he was not experienced enough for me to risk upsetting him about it, I let him move on. The pirouettes also became suddenly hazardous, and I felt him slip on one of them. We neared the end; the flying changes were coming. I headed him across the diagonal, one two, two two, three two, four two, five two, six two, seven two, eight two, nine two! We had completed without mistake the nine flying changes on every second stride. Again we had swung around to begin the second diagonal. One, two, three, four, five, six, seven, eight, nine, ten, eleven, twelve, thirteen, fourteen, fifteen! I breathed a sigh of relief when the difficult one-tempo changes were behind me. Bonheur had come through strongly once more and it was with much happiness and relief that we walked out of the ring. Half-laughing, half-crying, I could only whisper to the great horse that had seen me through to the end, "It's all over now, it's all over. . . ."

The world came into focus again. I dismounted happily. The test was not perfect, but I was very happy with it.

The soggy ground had spoiled the piaffe for almost all horses. My ride had compared favourably with the rides of other participants, I was told. People congratulated me as I moved to sit down on a spectators' bench. Now I was able to catch my breath, contemplate the test just finished, and wait to hear what my marks had been. Emily had taken Bonheur to cool him out.

The few Canadians who had come all the way to Tokyo to watch the equestrian activities gathered around me as the judges began their consultation. They were quite hopeful for me, since one horse that had bucked in the ring had received a little over 700 marks, quite a good score that day. The judges were still talking, and I tried to guess what the gentlemen were saying as they fixed my fate. I have often thought that the lack of spectator appeal in dressage is due to the judging system and the amount of time it consumes. Half of the thrill of watching free skating is being able to see the marks go up immediately after each performance. The performance is still fresh in the mind, and after hearing the score, one can turn all one's attention to the next contestant. The lengthy consultations that dressage judges hold seem so unnecessary. All judges have been chosen for their ability to evaluate dressage. Why not let them arrive at their own scores and disclose them immediately after each test without consultation?

At any rate, my score of 549 finally went up on the board. Although I was not thrilled with it, I considered it another useful experience to add to my store of knowledge, and set off to see how my fellow athletes had fared.

Filatov was furious and did not hide it.

When the day was over he was standing third. Harry Boldt of Germany was leading with an exact ride and Henri Chammartin of Switzerland was second. On the second day, when a shorter test was ridden by the first six horses, the standings became official. The order had changed, with Chammartin winning the gold medal by one point over Boldt, and Filatov remaining third. In one judge's opinion Filatov was the winner, but the two others had marked him down.

I was repeatedly told by horsemen and spectators at the competition that I had been judged extremely hard, but that at my age I could not expect it to be otherwise. In the long run it would be a blessing. I had a future in riding ahead of me, and a victory too soon would kill the flower before it had reached full bloom.

After my marks went up, Inez Fischer Credo said: "I have done lots of judging myself, and I watched your ride closely. I thought you would be at least 100 points above me." I was extremely happy that I had come only 40 points below her.

After his ride on the second day I bumped into Filatov. Throwing an arm around me, he pulled me towards the indoor riding ring, far from the Grand Prix scene. "Saddle your horse," he said. "I want to ride him. Now."

The rain drummed on the metal roof, and distantly audible were the sounds of the Grand Prix spectators leaving the Olympic grounds. Filatov stood holding Bonheur while I made adjustments to the saddlery. The atmosphere in the arena was dull and grey, the windows high up on the walls affording little light. We three were off by ourselves, away from horses schooling for the next day's jumping event.

The anger had left the Russian now: it did not matter anymore. No human opinion could really affect his passion for the art he loved and lived. I knew that his soul sang as he prepared to mount my horse. And how Bonheur came to life, piaffing and passaging, snorting fire through his dilated nostrils, while I looked on inspired.

Getting down to the more technical aspects of it, Filatov explained carefully what he had done to make the horse react the way he did. I made mental notes of all he said. Soon Filatov motioned me to mount, and started to school me up and down one side of the arena, making sure I had grasped what he had shown me.

Mother, who had just reached the spectators' gallery in time to see the lesson, thanked Filatov for helping me. His eyes smiled encouragingly when he said, "One more year and Bonheur is. . . ." and he made a gesture with his hand supposed to mean something marvellous. As Emily took the dripping wet Bonheur from me, I stood watching Filatov disappear through the doorway, still every inch the conquerer. He paused for a moment, before he walked out into the rain.

As I watched him go, I promised myself: "I am going to ride, ride, ride. I am in love with it. I have seen the masters, talked with them, and been trained by them. I will cherish the experience of these last few weeks all my life long. I now understand that the Olympics is not a goal in itself, it is not the end. It is a beginning."

Appendix: A free dancer's approach to dressage

What I had learned of the science and psychology of movement in Mother's dance classes helped me to understand classical equestrian doctrine. A fascinating parallel can be drawn between the art of riding and the art of free dance: both aim at restoring the purity of natural movement. The natural movements of the horse suffer from the rider's weight and sometimes his wrong influences. The natural movements of man have been all but destroyed by the conditions of civilization, with its sedentary occupations.

The horse, not meant to bear a weight upon his back, tenses as soon as he is mounted. From a muscular point of view, he "falls apart," or *disconnects* the forehand from the hindquarters. The result is a hollow back and unco-ordinated, stiff, cramped gaits. To ride a horse so that he moves his body as a whole, united or *collected*, as if he were free and riderless, is the art of dressage.

Just as dressage aims at uniting the hindquarters of the horse with the forehand, so free dance aims at connecting the lower part of the human body, the pelvis, with the upper part, the trunk. This is accomplished by the back-muscle action called the *pelvic tilt·* The pelvic tilt, achieved simply by

129

bracing the back, is the basis for moving the body as a whole.

It is in the lumbar region, or small of the back, that natural movement originates. Here are the main springs, the muscles of the small of the back. The tightening of these muscles, in free dance called the *central contraction of the spine*, is a prerequisite for all natural movement. Every natural movement, small or large, originates from the lumbar region and extends from there in collaboration with the rest of the anatomy to the farthest units, giving man complete control over his whole body.

In learning to move naturally as a free dancer, I soon realized that a harmonious walk, uniting all members of the body, is an art. I will try to describe the technique of the natural, free walk in slow motion.

Each step begins with bracing the back, whereby the pelvis is raised at the front where the hip bones are, and lowered at the rear. The bracing of the back, extending upwards and downwards into the central contraction of the spine, affects the neck- and leg-muscles. The neck-muscle action raises the chin slightly above the horizontal and shortens the back of the neck. The leg-muscle action bends the knee of the moving leg, which results in the raising of the heel and the dropping of the toe. As the foot thus moves over the ground, the body passes vertically above it. While the centre of gravity is transferred in the direction of the forward movement, the foot rolls from toe to heel on the ground. The step completed, the knee of the moving leg and the neck are again passively stretched, restoring the chin to the horizontal position. The whole procedure is repeated as the muscles of the lumbar region contract again and so create the *impulse* for the next step. I say "create" because natural movement is not a simple, instinctive functioning, as can be observed in the plant or animal order.

It is an expression, through the activity of the body, of an intellectual perception.

Technically defining the free walk, one can say that it is a circular, rise-and-fall motion of the human body in the forward direction, in which contraction and release, activity and passivity, alternate. This is the principle of perpetual motion, from the simple contractions of the amoeba to the complicated combinations of a free dancer's and rider's movement. In the free walk, the contraction-and-release motion of the spine results in a "swinging back," causing all joints of the body to bend and stretch, contract and relax. This action gives elasticity, spring and elevation to the movement of the walker, as he steps *over*, not *into*, the ground.

The same principle underlies the free walk of a horse. Starting from the hindquarters, the main source of power, the horse contracts from rear to front, creating the same effects that characterize the free walk of a man: the swinging back and the relaxed action of the knees, ankles, head and neck.

When a man so rides a horse that his centre of gravity coincides with that of his mount, he is in perfect balance and rhythm. The unity of both bodies in every movement is expressed in the quiet harmony of the whole carriage of the horse. The feeling of complete understanding between man and mount can be compared with artistic ballroom dancing, wherein each partner finds equal pleasure in both leading and following the other. However, since single members of the body can move independently from the rest, movement can also be "disconnected," that is, with limbs moving in different directions.

In contrast with natural movement, disconnected or *peripheral* movement may, anatomically, start anywhere. Without the central contraction of the spine, the modern man on the move walks like a puppet or robot. Legs move from the hips, feet land heels first. Static, even in motion, the disconnected walk is a succession of steps with the weight always maintained on the back foot, the one that is not actively engaged; whereas the free walk is an uninterrupted movement in which the weight of the body is continually transferred from the back to the front foot. On foot as well as on horseback, the disconnected walk can be recognized by a dragging of the legs, because the movement is not supported by the action of the lumbar region, from where the impulse comes. The result is a tense walk that is an imitation of free motion, lacking the impulsion, continuity, swing and follow-through so characteristic of natural movement.

When the rider's back and that of the horse swing in *rhythm*, both are relaxed, or *supple*, a fact which is manifested in the harmonious *contact* between the rider's hands and the horse's mouth. This contact is in no way forced, but results from the horse stretching his neck forward and down in search of the rider's hand. This moment is perhaps one of the most exciting in the relationship between horse and rider, since it proves that the horse has come to trust its rider and co-operates with him by free will. The animal no longer fears that an awkward movement on the rider's part will jerk his mouth, and consequently follows the rider's influences with the confidence of a ballroom dancer who knows there is no danger of being stepped upon by her partner.

The relaxed swinging of the rider's spine extending itself into the horse's back not only maintains rhythm, but also causes the horse's hind legs to track supply and energetically into the direction of the corresponding forelegs. Now the elements of *rhythm, suppleness, contact,* and *straightness* are important aspects of *collection*: the ideal posture of horse and rider in motion. The horse's back appears to become shorter; it changes its carriage in correspondence to the degree of collection. The smallest degree of collection is intended just to hold the horse together in the forward motion, as in the free walk, trot or canter across country. Increased degrees of collection transform the movement into proper *collected gaits*. In advanced dressage collection, the horse's centre of gravity moves from the forehand ever nearer to the hindquarters, so that in the end the relieved forehand is automatically raised and the horse can almost trot on the spot, as in the piaffe—or eventually carry its whole weight on the hind legs, as in the levade.

When horse and rider move as one unit as described before, the rider is said to "follow the horse's movements." Failing to do this, he "stays behind." Horse and man become separate entities, with the latter having to clamp on with his legs, bumping in the saddle all the while.

Dressage training should always be directed to the whole horse, because no one can ever arrive at collection by working on separate parts of the anatomy. Yet the mistake is often made of trying to imitate the picture of a collected horse, by, for example, rounding his neck with the reins. These misunderstandings occur when the rider has no notion of how to collect *himself* in motion. The rider himself should undergo a training course in free movement. Only when he is relaxed will the contraction of the spine affect the head position and shorten and stretch the back of the neck with every movement.

In contrast to the "chair" seat, the dressage rider balances on the crotch and the two seat bones. To develop the muscles for this position, which is quite painful in the beginning, the rider should kneel with closed and later with spread knees on the ground. Holding his spine completely straight, he should "ride" in the posting movement. The muscle pains resulting from doing this simple exercise properly for a few minutes exceed the aches that a whole day of walking would produce in one's legs. Learning to "post" on the ground to music develops a feeling for rhythm, without which a rider can eventually destroy the individual rhythm of his horse.

It was the music theorist Jaques-Dalcroze who discovered one of the secrets of Greek education, that rhythm is *physiological*. Rhythm cannot be intellectually conceived, it has to be *felt*. In free dance the faculty of co-ordination between mind and body is developed by learning to move from the lumbar region. Loosening and strengthening exercises prepare the muscles for instantaneous elastic and dynamic action.

The rider who has undergone a thorough rhythmic training and has developed his own physical co-ordination and reaction will find his riding more pleasurable and will be able to adjust himself faster to the rhythm and cadences of the horse than someone with an untrained body. A rider who moves disconnected by himself cannot transmit connected, natural movement to his horse, because the tensions of his muscles work through the saddle into the horse's back and influence its gaits erroneously. In my own case I am certain that my free dance background saved me many hours that otherwise would have been spent in learning to adjust myself to the horse. Whoever does not believe this should see the same horse go under both a disconnected rider and a relaxed rider whose commands derive from central movement.

There are, and always will be, many different theories of riding. From Plato we learn that "the purpose of education is to give to the body and soul all the beauty and all the perfection of which they are capable." Applying the quotation to our subject, riding education must be intellectual and spiritual, as well as physical. Too often the tendency is to gear riding instruction to competitive performance, with the emphasis on technical skill only rather than the whole subject in all its aspects. The art of riding is superficially conceived of as technique. The instructor, concerned only with appearances, freezes the pupil into his concept of the "correct position" (Sit straight! Heels down! Elbows in! Hands three inches above the withers!) and expects the rider to move forward in this rigid fashion. Likewise may his colleague in dance order his pupil to stand in "position one," demanding that knees and feet be turned out, à la Charlie Chaplin, instead of face forward, according to the natural construction of the body. But the position of the limbs depends in dance on the way they are to execute a movement, and in riding on the manner in which they are to act upon a horse. To reverse the procedure, and start with the ultimate positions, with the consequence rather than the cause, leads in both dancing and riding to the cultivation of artificiality, and to mere craft, not art.

Genuine riding education appeals to the rider's intelligence. It explains the anatomy and laws of locomotion of the horse. It points out how the horse reacts to different pressures and why, thereby explaining how to influence him at the right moment to execute a required movement, giving the impression that the horse himself had made the decision that led to the movement. The object of dressage teachers should be to develop riding to the level of an art. The fact that some people cannot distinguish art from imitation does not alter the fact that the former achieves perfection, whereas the latter only imitates perfection; which brings us to the subject of judging.

Too many judges, whether amateur or professional, evaluate dressage without a sixth sense: the kinaesthetic, or movement-feeling, sense. They think that dressage comprises only those movements that can be seen. But motion should not merely be seen, it should be felt. Dressage enthusiasts must be able to perceive the movements as if they themselves were executing them. For example, the collection of a horse cannot be judged by looking at his head and neck carriage alone, for as I have mentioned before, there are numerous ways to round a horse's neck artificially with the reins.

Presented as an endless sequence of different, difficult steps, dressage must become boring to the uninitiated. This may account for its lack of popularity with the public, in comparison with jumping. The Biblical saying that "the Spirit giveth life," whereas "the letter killeth," also holds true here. Executed as an art, with an almost spiritual fluidity and grace, dressage never fails to impress even the layman at any time. There should be that same plastic phrasing that we find in dance, that continuous movement expressing continuous life, animated by thought.

To help riders train their horses in the correct way, national dressage tests should be so written as to stress the important foundation work.

Starting with the *preliminary* division, horses ought to be judged almost solely on their rhythm and steadiness of performance. Head carriage and collection should be ignored. The horse that exhibits the best natural gaits and is moving at an even tempo at all times should get the highest points.

The tests on the *novice* level should encourage the same ideas as the preliminary, adding a few simple figures that judges could watch for obedience and suppleness. Big circles and figure eights with periodical halts are good exercises for horses at this stage of development. I am against asking for strong trots and canters, because these cannot be achieved without proper collection, which novice horses should not be expected to exhibit.

The *elementary* level should show the horse beginning to balance himself and accept work on the bit. In a free forward movement, the rider must drive the hindquarters well forward; the impulse comes from the rider's back and legs, producing a swing and liveliness of pace which attest to a supple back and the horse's accepting the bit. The first loosening exercises, consisting of bending and flexing, can now be introduced, serving as a preparation for all two-track movements. To these belong "yielding to the rider's leg," and "shoulder-in," as well as turns on the forehand and changes of tempo from ordinary to strong gaits.

Only at the *intermediate* level should the horse be asked to be properly collected. This requires the ability to hold himself in balance while changing tempo and gait. Some advanced suppling exercises, comprising counter-canter and serpentines, voltes and half-voltes, can be demanded at this level. Also a number of rein-backs, with the horse being asked to trot right on from the rein-back. It would be wrong to use a double bridle at this stage, for it would tend to overflex the young horse. The two-track movements should be restricted to "shoulder-in," "yielding to the rider's leg," and perhaps only in the advanced stages of the intermediate level, half-passes in walk and trot.

The jump from the intermediate to the *medium* division is to my mind the crucial one. The horse is now asked to perform by international rules, i.e. in a large 20 x 60 metre ring, and on a simple double bridle. Besides correctness and precision in all movements, judges must now ask for ever-increasing impulsion, fluidity and brilliance. All two-track movements, including renvers, travers and half-passes must be mastered, as well as a flying change, done on the diagonal, or on a serpentine. This is the last test on the national level, for hereafter the horse graduates to the Prix St. Georges, first of the F. E. I. (Federation Equestre Internationale) international tests. The second hardest international test is the Intermediare, after which comes the Grand Prix de Dressage, the highest test of horsemanship in the world. This test includes the flying change every stride, the piaffe and the passage.

The reaching of this level is by no means the end of the road. The art lies in perfecting the movements and making horse and rider exact and yet brilliant. The art also encompasses the ability to bring horses of different types and temperaments to the same high level of achievement. Every horse brings with it new problems, new excitements, and an ever increasing awareness of one's own limitations. And although one may make mistakes out of ignorance or lack of technical ability, the rider who aspires to true art will always keep the well-being of the horse itself in mind. He will never forget this quotation from the Count de Souza: "Horsemanship is sometimes brought into disrepute because those interested in it fail always to keep in mind that being a horseman means having the honour to be the friend and master of one of God's most noble creatures."

Glossary of dressage terms

Aids: the communication between rider and horse.

Central Movement: movement of the whole or any part of the body that originates in the "centre of the body"—the small of the back. All movement must originate in this area in order to achieve perfect balance and harmony of motion.

Collection: co-ordination of the parts of the horse to achieve harmonious movements. The hindquarters must be brought well under to lighten the forehand. Collection is essential for central movement in the horse.

Extension: a lengthening of stride without increasing the tempo of the gait.

Flying Change: the change of lead at the canter in one stride without varying the tempo or the pace.

Half-pass: an exercise in which the horse moves diagonally on "two tracks" flexed in the direction of the movement. (See "*Two-Track Movements*")

Impulsion: controlled or potential energy necessary to achieve brilliance in all movements of dressage.

Lead: at the start of each stride in the canter the horse must lead with his inside hind leg. Hence the terms "right lead" and "left lead."

Longeing: suppling the horse by working him from the ground in both directions on a circle at the end of a longe rein.

Longe Rein: usually a canvas rein about thirty feet in length fixed with a spring clip, or the equivalent, at one end.

139

Passage: a forward movement produced by the powerful push-off of the diagonal pairs of legs, in the phase sequence of the trot, giving the impression of suspended forward movement.

Piaffe: sustained trotting action with almost no forward movement.

Pirouette: circular movement on "two tracks" with a radius equal to the length of the horse, the forehand moving around the haunches. The hind legs must maintain the tempo of the gait while acting as the pivot of the movement.

Renvers: a "two-track" movement along the wall with the haunches pushed out to the wall. Only the hind legs cross in this exercise. (See *Travers*)

Shoulder-in: a "two-track" movement in which the horse's neck is flexed away from the direction of movement. Only the forelegs cross in this exercise.

Single-Track Movements: movements in which the hind legs step into the track made by the forelegs.

Travers: a "two-track" movement along the wall with the haunches pushed away from the wall. Only the hind legs cross in this exercise. (See *Renvers*)

Two-Track Movements: movements in which the hind legs tread a separate line which is parallel to the track made by the forelegs.

Volte: a circle 6 metres in diameter. This is the smallest circle a horse can negotiate while remaining on one track.